# The
# Day
# the
# War
# Ended

# JACKY HYAMS

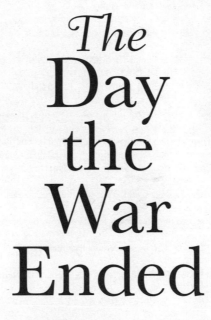

# The Day the War Ended

*Untold true stories
from the last days
of the War*

JOHN BLAKE

Published by John Blake Publishing,
an imprint of Bonnier Books UK
80-81 Wimple Street
London
W1G 9RE

www.facebook.com/johnblakebooks
twitter.com/jblakebooks

First published in paperback in 2020

Paperback ISBN: 9781789463392
Ebook ISBN: 9781789463507
Audiobook ISBN: 9781789463484

British Library Cataloguing-in-Publication Data:

A catalogue record for this book is available from the British Library.

Design by www.envydesign.co.uk

Printed and bound in Great Britain by Clays Ltd, Elcograf S.p.A.

1 3 5 7 9 10 8 6 4 2

John Blake Publishing is an imprint of Bonnier Books UK
www.bonnierbooks.co.uk

# CONTENTS

# AUTHOR'S NOTE

Before 1971 the pound was divided into 20 shillings (s). One shilling was made up of 12 pennies (d). A pound was made up of 240 pennies. A guinea was worth 21 shillings or 1 pound and 1 shilling (£1 1s 0d).

I have given prices and sums of money in the original pre-decimal currency, which was replaced in February 1971.

In order to calculate today's value of any original price quoted, the National Archives has a very useful website with a currency converter: http://www.nationalarchives. gov.uk/currency-converter

As a general rule of thumb, £1 in 1945 was worth about £43 in today's currency.

# THE DAY WAR ENDED

He was a stranger. He lived permanently on the mantel-piece. Like millions of other kids' dads, in the summer of 1945 when World War II ended, my father was an absent presence in our home until the day of his return from far-off India in the summer of 1946.

'That's your daddy,' children all over the country would be told, families pointing to the man in uniform, proudly staring into the camera, maybe a written scrawl on the back of the black-and-white photo carefully forwarded home with a long-awaited letter.

Perhaps, I would reflect many decades later, the reason I had been unable to bond with my dad following the separation of those early toddler years lay buried in the conflict of my subsequent unhappy relationship with him. Who could ever know for sure if the long wartime absence of fathers through World War II permanently affected their children's subsequent relationship with them? And what of the children who never met the man in the photo because he had been killed? How would they fare beyond the family's loss?

Each family in Britain has a different story to tell about this war that had made such a huge impact on their lives. Many stories were far more dramatic or damaging than mine. Like so much about the after-effects of World War II, the emotional impact of families being torn apart or evacuated elsewhere or losing loved ones could not be explored fully until decades later.

These stories were amongst the many issues surrounding the advent of the war's end. In looking closely at the period in Britain's history when World War II ended, firstly on VE Day (Victory in Europe), when the war between the Allied and Axis powers and Hitler's Germany formally ended on 8 May 1945, to be followed later that summer by VJ Day (Victory over Japan), with Japan's unconditional surrender to the Allies on 15 August 1945, after the news that atomic bombs had been dropped on Hiroshima and Nagasaki (6 August), those two dates in the summer of 1945 seem the most significant guides to the era. (Just over a year later came an official Allied Victory Parade in London on 6 June 1946, a huge military event marking the cessation of hostilities.)

But in marking how the official ending of World War II was experienced for those millions at home – nine-tenths of the population of Great Britain had remained civilians –

when the five and a half long years of war formally ceased, was it even possible to highlight a specific or fixed point in time when wartime finally, irrevocably, ended in Britain? Or had too much changed with day-to-day lives to bring forth any easy answer?

One can, of course, acknowledge the dates in the calendar as victory and leave it at that, paying due homage to those who perished. According to the Royal British Legion, World War II killed 382,700 members of the British Armed Forces and 67,100 civilians. As tragic as each death impacts on every home, this figure seems relatively low when balanced against World War II's impact on the tens of millions who perished from other countries around the world. Such histories, of course, did not emerge immediately. They would be gradually revealed to the world in the months and years that followed that iconic official VE Day.

The complexities of war ending in Britain were very far from simple: a small country with a vast empire sprawled across the globe, an island separated from the rest of Europe by water, unconquered by an evil force, yet torn apart both economically and in bricks and rubble, all this in addition to the long-lasting emotional strife of those at home living right through the war with their the stories of hardship, family separation, injury and, in some cases, devastation.

Then there is the ironic case of Britain's leadership through the tough times until the final ending. You'd expect such an individual to emerge as a feted colossus hailed by the people when the hostilities stopped. Not quite.

Even now Winston Churchill remains a legendary icon (if controversial to some). Back in 1945, he had been viewed as a political giant, a tubby man of privilege with a cigar and a V-sign who had steered the nation through the most fearsome days and nights with memorable rhetoric.

'You do your worst and we will do our best,' he wrote in July 1941 following one of many visits to bomb-damaged cities like Plymouth where the sight of the streets, ragged from destruction, brought tears to his eyes.

Yet Winston Churchill and his Conservative Party were soundly rejected by the British people when nearly 25 million war-weary voters turned up at the ballot box in the July 1945 election that tumultuous summer to vote in favour of the Labour Party. It was headed by the man who had been Churchill's deputy prime minister from 1942 onwards, Clement Attlee.

That sudden dismissal of Churchill, unexpected as it was at the time, revealed the depth of the struggle endured by the millions who had lived through wartime.

They'd come through, got on with it stoically – somehow. Yet many hungered for change, aware that the years ahead for the victorious country meant facing up to huge problems. Millions had urgent need of housing thanks to the overall requirement to rebuild the damaged country. On the economic scale, the country was broken, in huge debt to its major ally, the United States. Even many of Britain's Armed Forces, fearful of the years of disillusion and unemployment that had followed the First World War, voted for a new Labour government – and the impact of serious political change. Normal party politics had been suspended from May 1940 to May 1945 in the interest of national unity when the three main political parties had formed a wartime coalition.

Now it was the turn of a new kind of leadership.

Women's wartime battle had been, for most, on the ground, though there had been valiant and courageous effort from the comparatively small numbers of women in the Forces, the 1 million-plus female factory workers as well as the huge army of female volunteers on the ground.

Most of those wives and mothers, exhausted and weary, saw a glimmer of hope for the future in a new socialist-led Labour offer of social security for all, family allowances, educational reform and a brand new National Health Service.

For even as victory had been claimed, there was a growing, uneasy sense that peace, in the future, would not resemble anything that anyone might have once hoped for or imagined. No chance whatsoever of turning the clock back to any semblance of previously held stability. Too much had been lost.

Yet the British sense of humour, never far from the surface, was poised to sum up any underlying cynicism of the days ahead. 'Well, there's nothing to look forward to now. There was always the all-clear before,' quipped BBC Radio comedian Robb Wilton in his sketch 'The Day Peace Broke Out'. (Wilton, 1881–1957), was one of BBC Radio's most popular comedians in World War II thanks to his series of sketches and monologues loved by millions of listeners.)

Peace proved itself as a somewhat complicated arrival. Many could still recall the untruthful (or fake news) 'peace in our time' story the newspapers promised the country back in 1938 after Prime Minister Neville Chamberlain's return from his disastrous encounter with Hitler in Munich. A year later, the 'peace' had morphed into war. Real war.

GERMANY CAPITULATED! crowed the *Daily Telegraph* newspaper on 8 May 1945. Here, at long last, came the real event, finally arriving after all the excitement at home of June 1944's D-Day Normandy landings in Europe, followed by the nail-biting momentum of the long months that followed as the Allied incursion into Europe fought German military determination – and drove it towards victory.

But how could it be peace as we'd understand it now? The ink was barely dry on the surrender treaties signed and the armaments only just laid down. Relief for the moment was the only order of the day. Yet the word 'peace' glossed over the reality of that crowing headline. The Allied victory had not always been a certainty.

On 27 March 1945, the last German V-2 rocket had landed in England in Orpington, Kent, killing one person and injuring thirty. Earlier that same day, another lethal V-2 rocket had exploded in London's East End, killing 134 residents of Hughes Mansions, Vallance Road.

In the months before those last V-2s, many thousands had died and families shed bitter tears as a result of the German 'last-ditch' attempt to destroy Allied cities.

Yet just weeks after those last rockets, people of all ages were dancing, cheering, revelling in the streets everywhere. Could Britain swiftly pick up the pieces of life after five and a half years of determined and repeated battering from the enemy? Over time, yes. But it was never going to be a swift return to normality.

The end story itself was a slow, gradual finale for those at home. 'Half lighting', as it was officially described, came to millions of blacked-out homes in Britain as far back as September 1944. Other than for those living on the coast, 'windows, other than skylights, need be curtained only sufficiently to prevent objects inside the building from being distinguishable from outside'.

Direct lights were still forbidden and, if the warning siren sounded, 'half lighting' or 'dim out' became black-out again if the air-raid siren sounded. Regulations were slightly relaxed on car and cycle lamps and better street lighting was allowed, provided it could be turned off during raids. By December 1944, lighting on buses and trains was close to normal again, and churches with stained-glass windows could have their pre-war lights on. By 30 December, car owners were told they could light up their number plates again.

It was not until 20 April 1945 that Herbert Morrison, the then home secretary, announced in the House of Commons (to loud cheering) the total abolition of the blackout from dusk on Monday 24 April, except for an area five miles inland from the coast. This last restriction was finally lifted on 10 May.

Yet the delight of taking down the blackout curtaining or dismantling the damp and disliked Anderson shelter sunk into the garden proved to be minor enthusiasms after all that had gone before. Often, households were frequently shabby behind the blackout curtains, with faded casement curtains and lace curtains rotting.

Tearing down the curtains could be a dirty process. One Devon woman found only dust and dead insects accumulated behind the shutters for six years. Thrift, not surprisingly, had taken over the country as a national obsession. One Midlands woman reported afterwards: 'We did not go mad and burn the materials; they came in useful for years.'

Children too had an unexpected reaction to the dramatic turning on of light. Many young children, never allowed out after dark for their entire lifetime, wept in fear when taken out to see the lights.

One child, taken out by her mother to see the hitherto unseen moon responded: 'What's that lamp doing in the sky?'

Two weeks after the formal abolition of the blackout, a new order came through: floodlighting and decorative lighting on seaside piers and bandstands was banned to save fuel. Austerity had only removed its hat very briefly. It would remain a byword for the country for several years to come.

Consider what the country looked like in that momentous summer of 1945.

Three quarters of a million houses had been destroyed or severely damaged. Public services, disrupted all the time by war, continued to be hugely disrupted for some time. Life expectancy had increased (from just fifty years in early 1900 to around age sixty-five). But access to medical services was, mostly, far from free – millions were too impoverished to pay for them.

Efforts to improve lives had been made pre-war: the late 1930s had seen a healthy slum clearance programme until war halted it. As a consequence there remained many appalling Victorian slums in the big cities and over-crowded, inadequate and now ruined housing across the country. Seven million homes lacked a supply of hot water. Six million homes relied on an outside toilet.

The year 1945, so momentous in its historical status, was a very different kind of 'victory'. Technically, the war had been won by Britain and its Allies. But the reality of retrieving even some part of the ease and comfort of peacetime emerged as a lengthy process.

It was long acknowledged by the authorities that the British public would deserve a new start when war ended. In December 1942, the Beveridge Report was published, drawn up by economist Sir William Beveridge. The report proposed a comprehensive post-war system of social security for Britain. Essentially this lay the foundation of the welfare state, attacking the evils of want, disease, ignorance, squalor and idleness.

At the time, the report caused a sensation. A popular version sold over 600,000 copies.

Then, as war began to draw to a close in 1944, more government directives set forth two major developments: a White Paper committed the government to the pursuit of full employment, followed by a new 1944 Education Act, creating free, non-fee-paying grammar schools and free, compulsory secondary education to age fifteen, providing chances of a social mobility, via university, that had never existed. (Until that time the standard school-leaving age was fourteen.)

Furthermore, that year's new Town and Country Planning Act gave far-reaching powers to local authorities to acquire bomb-damaged areas for reconstruction and redevelopment.

But in those few weeks prior to the official ending, the beginnings of a huge and dramatic scenario engulfed the world.

On 12 April 1945, as Franklin D Roosevelt, president of the United States – and a great wartime ally of Britain and then prime minister Winston Churchill – died, members of Germany's Hitler Youth distributed cyanide capsules to the audience seated at Berlin's Philharmonic, as they watched the final concert of the Nazi era. The curtain was finally coming down for Hitler and the Nazi regime.

Three days later Allied soldiers encountered appalling scenes of horror as they liberated the concentration camp of Bergen-Belsen. Millions had been murdered systematically in other concentration camps, and many sent to die in gas chambers.

At the end of April, holed up in his Berlin bunker with his new wife, Eva Braun, Adolf Hitler used a gun and a cyanide capsule to end it all.

That same April, the UK's Labour Party issued its end of war manifesto which included an urgent housing programme, the creation of a new National Health Service and the nationalisation of many key industries. Events in that month had been moving incredibly swiftly – but the politicians believed that the building blocks were now in place to steer the country towards the new start everyone deserved.

If the real changes to everyday lives were to limp along slowly, it is important to consider Britain just as it was in the year of 1945.

There were trains, trams, buses, tubes and a few taxis on the road in the cities. In the country, bikes were the most frequent mode of transport. Car ownership, pre-war, had been for the well off. Compared to what lay ahead it was very low. Walking some distance wasn't a weekend hobby, it was frequently a daily necessity.

On the streets many people wore hats – the men politely doffing them to the women and carefully walking on the outside of the pavement.

Culturally, books, films and plays were at the mercy of the censor. And foreigners, any kind, were not yet welcome.

('No Irish, no blacks, no dogs' was a sign frequently seen by those searching for somewhere to live in post-war British cities; you could even read the mantra, or something similar, in the classified ads of newspapers.)

Divorce increased after 1945 yet for some years it remained a social disgrace. Ditto for children born out of wedlock. Regular churchgoing remained an important part of many lives yet marriage, for many, remained a lifetime sentence: more drudgery, less joy. Women now worked, after achieving a measure of wartime independence, but equality between the sexes was still some way ahead. The word 'teenager' did not exist.

Despite the huge changes to lives wrought by war, Britain was still very much a class-bound society, separated by class and politics. Yet the country, rich or poor, retained an enormous pride in Britain, a society united by war, a common cause.

The country had stood alone for a whole year, as Winston Churchill reminded the celebrating crowds on VE Day. That counted for so much. Reverence for royalty remained as it was, mostly thanks to the wartime newsreel and newspaper events of the royal family diligently 'doing their bit'.

At the end of the day, it was a conservative land in 1945 that faced the uncertainty of the future. Yet the people remained steadfast in their belief in the values of their country, as resolute as they'd been throughout the long years of war.

'Four things saved us,' wrote the *Manchester Guardian* that day. 'The English Channel; the combined prowess of the

Navy and the RAF; Mr Churchill's leadership. The fourth was something in the national character which refused to take in the staring prospect of defeat.'

And now, as I complete this introduction, Britain is in the midst of a global pandemic. A war with a deadly virus, COVID-19, has created havoc around the world.

Millions of British people have been facing the most stringent government restrictions between each other and their way of life since those wartime years and VE Day.

Yet that same national character and strength of purpose has re-emerged, resonant and powerful. All those years later it reveals a people united, resilient, mindful of the need to support each other in the face of a terrible adversity, determined, yet again, to refuse to broker defeat – of any description.

The link between Britain's past and the present day has not been broken.

# CHAPTER 1

# THE BEGINNING
# OF THE END

*'The world must know what happened*
*– and never forget.'*
GENERAL EISENHOWER

The first turning point towards the end of the war came in
June 1944 (D-Day) when the Allied forces landed 150,000
troops on the beaches of Normandy, France. This was the
largest seaborne invasion in history. Two months later, Paris
was liberated after four years of Nazi occupation. For those
at home, it looked as if Germany was being forced back on
many fronts.

January 1945 saw everyone's hopes begin to rise further
for the end of wartime hostilities, although the five and a
half years of shortages and deprivation were very much still
part of day-to-day life.

Joan Strange, from Worthing, was a physiotherapist in her thirties. Her tireless efforts to help those escaping the Nazi regime before the war and her subsequent work to help refugees in post-war Europe and South East Asia proved to be a lifelong commitment. In her diary she recorded major World War II events throughout the war as well as details of local shortages and events.

## 1 January

Things do seem to be hastening towards the end of the war. In the West the Allies have regained about a third of the ground lost to the Nazi counter-offensive. Lemons are on sale in the town and the last of the barbed wire on the Worthing Parade is being removed by soldiers. It's been there for more than four years and looks very rusty. The cold spell has ended.

## 10 January

Petrol can be bought at any garage again. Field Marshal Montgomery has been given command of ALL Allied armies on the north side of the German-held area.

He has re-established confidence. The Germans are doing their best to split the Allies with broadcasts purporting to come from the BBC which contain high praise for Monty and reviling the American troops in the Ardennes battle.

## 21 January

My neighbour has sawn up her air-raid shelter wood supports as there is no coal.

Another difficulty: having to use only five coupons on a pair of shoes, everyone has their foot gear mended until the shoes end. I shot into Watts today [Watts was a well-known family-run shoe shop in Worthing] to retrieve a pair and to leave behind those I was wearing! Shopping is difficult. The Burma Road has been reopened.

## 24 January

We had a Refugee Committee meeting today to discuss plans for coping with hundreds of war-shocked, badly nourished Dutch children. It looks as if the German children are in a similar plight. These are the children who will be forming the post-war world – will their experiences make for better international relations or will their terrible times hinder friendly overtures? Mother made some real Seville orange marmalade today – the first for several years. Many people can't spare any sugar for it, so the oranges still look plentiful in the shop windows, even though the supply arrived two days ago.

[Joan's awareness of the stream of war-shocked, poorly nourished children in Europe was shared by many millions in Britain reading the newspaper reports of the desperate food situation in countries like France, Holland and Belgium. In February 1945, hundreds of British families offered to house some of these Dutch children whose plight was heartbreaking – a few of the youngest ones, arriving in Britain and faced with newspaper reporters, thought the press photographers, levelling their cameras to record their arrival, were a firing squad.]

## 25 January

Mr Bevin, Minister for Labour, has estimated that the artificial ports used in the Normandy landings must have saved between 100,000 and 150,000 British and American casualties.

## 30 January

The Russians are only ninety miles from Berlin. Terrible conditions reign in Germany – millions evacuating out of Berlin and millions trekking into the capital from invaded German territory. Intense cold worsens the conditions for these wretched civilians – Nazi authorities continually beg their people not to harass them by asking the whereabouts of relatives. The cold has been intense in Britain too. We ran out of fuel four days ago and I had to accept offers of logs and a bucket of coal from neighbours; we swapped the logs for two eggs and a packet of mixed fruit from Australia. A commando raid on a prison camp on the island of Luzon [home to Manila in the Philippines] freed 513 Allied prisoners captured by the Japs three years ago. Street lights were alight tonight for the first time since 1939.

## 11 February

The Black Sea Conference has ended. [Often known as the Yalta or Crimea Conference, this was the World War II meeting of the heads of government of Britain, the US and the Soviet Union to discuss the post-war reorganisation of Germany and Europe.] The points agreed upon have been broadcast. Germany is to be totally occupied and totally disarmed.

## 15 February

One of the greatest assaults of the war was launched against Germany by the Allied air forces in the last twenty-four hours. Over 2,750 heavy bombers smashed at strategic targets, mostly in support of the advancing Russian armies. Over 650,000 firebombs were dropped on Dresden alone.

## 20 February

Allied forces have smashed through the Siegfried Line [a German defensive line built in the 1930s] and are at the entrance to the Rhine Plain. Casualties are high on both sides. US planes have given Tokyo its biggest raid yet; parts of the city were still seen to be blazing from earlier raids. V-2s are still coming over here – chiefly in and around London.

## THE WEAPONS OF REVENGE

The flying bombs, V-1s and V-2s, were meant as Hitler's weapons of revenge, weapons Hitler boasted would win the war for Nazi Germany.

Not long after D-Day in June, London came under fire from V-1 flying bombs. These continued across London until October 1944 when the V-1 launch sites were captured while the Allies progressed through France and Belgium. The V-1s were pilotless aircraft that dropped to earth when their engines cut out, detonating an 1,800-pound warhead.

In September 1944, the V-2 rockets – the world's first long-range ballistic missiles – were launched against London and south-east England, killing 10,000 people and bringing a renewed evacuation from London by nearly a million families. These lethal weapons were also used to deadly effect in Belgium, France and the Netherlands. The V-2s could not be seen or heard in flight and they carried an even larger warhead of 2,200 pounds.

In March 1945, the rocket-launching sites in Northern France and Belgium were finally overrun by Allied forces, only weeks before hostilities in Europe finally ended.

The V-1 and V-2 rockets had been constructed by slave labour; tens of thousands of these workers died due to the appalling conditions in which they were held and forced to work by Germany.

Like many Londoners, my mother and her family had fled the city for the second time as a consequence of the dreaded V-2s through the summer of 1944. My maternal grandparents, my aunts and my mother, then expecting my arrival, went to live in a rented house in a suburb of Leeds: I was born in the area as the year drew to a close. My father, serving with the Pay Corps, had been sent off to India earlier in 1944.

Typical of so many, our lives were topsy-turvy. Yet when tragedy struck, my mother's older sister, Sylvia, did not reveal to her Leeds-based family how her own life had been devastated that winter by a V-2 rocket. Married for just six months in early 1944 to an Austrian Jewish refugee, Otto Lobbenberg had been killed on leave in Antwerp, Belgium by a V-2 which exploded in the Rex Cinema on 16 December killing 567 soldiers and civilians, leaving nearly 300 injured.

Sylvia did not reveal this to anyone in her family until after World War II had ended.

Jacky Hyams

Joan's diary continues:

### 25 February

Tokyo is continually being bombed. It looks as if the European and Pacific wars will end at the same time. Berlin has had its worst raid of the war – over half a million incendiaries and over 1,100 tons of high explosives. It must be terrible there.

### 6 March

The BBC reported that Mr Churchill has returned safely from a visit to Germany! He's the first British statesman to set foot there since Mr Chamberlain went to Munich six and a half years ago. The crossing of the Rhine will be a difficult task. But nothing will stop the Allies now.

The lifting of wartime restrictions in Worthing continues. Workmen are helping to remove the beach mines near the pier, the town hall clock is now illuminated, concrete anti-aviation devices are now being smashed up.

The chief difficulties remaining are the scarcity of fuel, queuing for fish, etc., lack of accommodation – all hotels are booked up fully for months ahead and some have dismissed their 'permanent' guests even, to make room for more.

The ration of fat is rather small and people try all sorts of dodges like using liquid paraffin for cake making – quite good too. MPs have found that housing is of greater concern to their constituents than any other post-war problem.

### 13 March

The Americans have thrown a pontoon bridge over the Rhine and troops are streaming across both the permanent and temporary bridges. The Germans have attacked the Remagen Bridge several times but only slight damage has been done. All the same, things are pretty hot there – a *Telegraph* reporter was killed yesterday while crossing in a jeep.

### 14 March

The German Commander-in-Chief of Berlin has ordered Berliners to 'fight to the last bullet'. Why the Nazis don't surrender we can't understand.

### 24 March

Field Marshal Montgomery's army is crossing the Rhine in strength. The leading newspaper article yesterday was titled: 'The Eve of the Heave'!

### 30 March

Good Friday. No papers today but everyone is listening to every wireless bulletin, just as we did in 1940. The great advance goes on. The Americans are closing the Ruhr trap on thousands of Nazis. It looks as if the Germans are clearing out of Holland – no rockets have come over for two days. Russians are crossing into Austria. The end is near!

In April, as people half expected to wake up to learn that the war in Europe was finally over and the British Army had swept into Germany at last, shelter and food became the important questions of the immediate future.

Yet the news on BBC Radio that American President Roosevelt died on 12 April somehow came as a personal shock to everyone. News came too that Allied troops were reported as being just fifteen miles from Berlin – yet the news of Roosevelt's death overwhelmed millions. In London, people stood on the streets staring unbelievably at the news-paper hoardings, even queuing up patiently for successive editions. Roosevelt's inspiring words of hope through the war had sustained the British people in the same way as Churchill's broadcasts.

English author Mollie Panter-Downes chronicled Roosevelt's death in her World War II book, *London War Notes*.

### 15 April

'Because the British have been prepared for the last few weeks to receive the good news which obviously nothing could spoil, the bad news knocked them sideways.

President Roosevelt's death came as a stupefying shock, even to those Britons whose idea of peace do not run much beyond the purely personal ones of getting their children home again, a roof back over their heads, a little car back on the road and plenty of consumer goods in the shops. To the more internationally minded, the news seemed a crushing disaster. People stood in the streets staring blankly at the first incredible newspaper headlines which appeared to have suddenly remodelled the architecture of the world. They queued up patiently for succeeding editions as if they hoped that something would be added to the first bald facts to make them more bearable. The flags hung limply at half mast along Whitehall, where knots of lugubrious people gathered at the entrance to Downing Street, hoping for a glimpse of Mr Churchill as he came back from adjourning the House of Commons' business of the day.

On the first shocked day after the president's death, one frequently heard the observation that at this juncture even Mr Churchill could almost have been better spared than Mr Roosevelt. It was a strange remark to hear in England, but it was a perfectly sincere one. The fact is that many people feel that the prime minister's supreme job was to steer this country safely through the Second World War, as it was the job of ... Lloyd George to steer it through the First World War.

Loyal and grateful Britons know that no other leader could have done it as well as Mr Churchill, but they believe that if, by sad chance, it had been he who had caused Friday's tragic headlines, England's post-war policy would have continued roughly on the same tracks. The post-war policy of a United States without Mr Roosevelt is hard to predict on this side of the Atlantic. People here might find comfort in the situation if they were at all familiar with the new president, but they are not.

The average Englishman, who knows little about American domestic politics, feels as lost as the average American would if Mr Churchill were to be suddenly succeeded by some relatively unknown Conservative. The evening papers came out with photographs and hastily dug up biographies of President Truman, which Londoners read non-committally. They glanced at the adjoining headlines, which said that Allied troops were reported only fifteen miles from Berlin, with ironically little apparent emotion and as though Berlin were a village on another planet. Mr Roosevelt's death will sober still more what would in any event have been a sober V-Day. The universal expression of profound personal sorrow, however, has far outweighed the sense of political uncertainty. No

> Briton has forgotten those dark times when the only cheerful thing seemed to be Mr Roosevelt's voice coming over the radio late at night and no Briton will ever forget. Elderly people with long memories say that they remember no such dazed outburst of general grief over the death of any other foreign statesman, or, for that matter, over many English ones. At the end of that sad Friday, innumerable people cancelled whatever plans they had made for the evening and stayed quietly at home because they had no heart for going out.
>
> It is all very different from what every one of us had expected the last few days of the European war to be like.'

A few days later came news of Nazi concentration camps where millions had been murdered. British forces had liberated Bergen-Belsen on 15 April. A BBC Radio broadcast by Richard Dimbleby revealed a horror hitherto unknown.

'The most horrible day of my life … no briefing had prepared me for this. I picked my way over corpse after corpse in the gloom … some of the poor starved creatures looked so utterly unreal and inhuman that I could have imagined that they had never lived at all.'

Later, newsreel cinemas showed film of the atrocities. Those departing the cinema came out in total shock. It didn't seem believable. Nonetheless, the overall focus for most in the country remained what they'd already experienced: the Blitz, the food shortages, the bombing raids, the shelters, the nightly blackout – all had left an indelible impression.

By the end of April, hearts lifted. The blackout had officially ended. The V-2s in the south-east had stopped for good. A lighted room could throw its brightness into the street without attracting the attention of an ARP (Air Raid Precautions) warden. On 2 May, news came that Berlin had surrendered to the Russians. Seriously good news to war ending was on its way, as Joan Strange recorded:

### 6 May

The leader in today's paper is titled 'Long Night Ended' and now that Hitler and Mussolini are dead [Hitler committed suicide on 30 April, Mussolini was executed by Italian partisans on 28 April] the paper ends: 'The monstrous fabric of their wicked ambitions had shrivelled up and at the end they were fugitives from justice – the world's justice. Would that the evil they did could be interred with their bones!

It lives after them and will long live: the ruin of their own countries, the destruction and desolation spread over Europe and far beyond its borders: the legacy of hate and things abominable which they bequeathed to their own people.'

The following day, 7 May, saw the official unconditional surrender of all German land, sea and air forces.

The surrender was to come into effect at fifty-nine minutes to midnight on 8 May.

## 7 May

At last the pronouncement has come! All day long everyone has been listening to the wireless and on the six o'clock news it was reported that tomorrow will be the official VE Day, although the surrender terms were signed by the Germans at 2.41am this morning in General Eisenhower's headquarters at Reims. The only Germans still fighting are those in Prague but that will cease soon. Allied ships are sailing into Oslo Fjord today. The bodies of Goebbels and his family have been found in Berlin; he poisoned his six children and ordered an SS guard to shoot himself and his wife. Hitler's body has not been found. Many important people have been liberated from Nazi prison; three former French premiers (Daladier, Blum and Reynaud), the Generals Gamelin and Weygand, Princess Mary's son and Pastor Niemöller, the anti-German pastor. He was held in Italy and was rescued by the Fifth Army; he'd been seven years in concentration camps.

Here in Worthing some flags have appeared in preparation for tomorrow, also a platform for the mayor to make his speech from outside the town hall (quite a number of people were sitting there from early afternoon waiting hopefully!). Aeroplanes have been doing their 'victory rolls' over the town and I'm sitting here at 11pm without the curtains being drawn!

## 8 May

It's come at last. I woke up at 7am to hear the sound of Mother wrestling with the flags (rather moth-eaten and patched relics of Queen Victoria's Jubilee!). But we weren't the first in the road after all as we were when Mussolini was captured in July 1943. The weather's been good for the first of the two VE holidays. It's been a queer sort of day, the highlights being the prime minister's short broadcast at 3pm and the King's at 9pm. The prime minister told huge crowds that gathered in Whitehall: 'This is your victory. In all our long history we have never seen a greater day than this.'

Hostilities cease officially at one minute past midnight tonight when it's hoped that any fighting against the Russians will cease. Mother and I listened to the thrilling broadcasts on the European victory. There were services in all churches and cinemas at 12pm today.

## 9 May

Today is still being celebrated as a public holiday – it's Russia's V-Day today.

At 8pm Marshal Stalin broadcast his victory message to his peoples. Quisling has given himself up. [Vidkun Quisling was the Norwegian army officer who collaborated with the Germans during their occupation of Norway. He was held responsible for sending nearly 1,000 Jews to die in concentration camps. He was executed by firing squad in October 1945.] Goering [the head of the

Luftwaffe] and Kesselring [the general in charge of all German forces in the south] have been captured. Prague is now entirely in Czech hands. The King and Queen have made a 'victory' tour of London's badly bombed East End. The German garrisons in the Atlantic French ports of Dunkirk, Lorient, St Nazaire and La Rochelle have surrendered to the French.

The public announcement of VE Day in Britain had turned into a nail-biting, behind-the-scenes delay while the victors argued about the exact timing of the announcement.

News came only when an American journalist based in Paris for the Associated Press news agency – a journalist who had already witnessed the historic signing of the German surrender at Reims – broke ranks to become the very first Allied journalist to break the VE Day story via the AP agency.

In New York, victory celebrations started. Then the British people were finally told that VE Day, 8 May, was theirs and that there would be a two-day public holiday, sharing their celebrations with their Allies, the Russians.

## 'THE COUNTRY WENT WILD'

Londoner Eva Merrill was seventeen and was working as a bank clerk in the City. Eva and her family were typical in that they had lived through a great deal in wartime, including evacuation from their home to the countryside, then a return back to London.

# THE DAY THE WAR ENDED

By Christmas 1944 we felt the end was in sight, although sporadic attacks from V-1s and V-2s continued until March 1945. We all carried on, but the country was very tired after nearly six years of war. Shortages and rationing, towns and villages devastated by bombing, families split up, to say nothing of the personal heartbreak suffered by those bereaved through acts of war. We were all ground down and drained and though we knew it could not be much longer before this awful war was finished, these last months dragged on interminably.

In the spring of 1945 the government had lifted the blackout restrictions.

This gave everybody a great boost. Not to have to cover every chink of light at night when drawing the curtains and to have street lights again was wonderful. A cigarette could be lit in the street without a warden shouting, 'Put that light out!' Kerbs and steps could be seen and not tripped over. Little things but they meant a lot to us.

At the end of April news arrived that one million German troops had surrendered in Italy and Austria. Berlin then fell on 7 May and the unconditional surrender of Germany was announced.

The country went wild, dancing and parties on every street. Bonfires were lit, bands played and pubs were thrown open. We had never experienced anything like it before. It was all so spontaneous, a great shouting of joy from one end of the country to the other.

I went up to the West End of London, along with a crowd of bank colleagues, and we danced along the pavement, streamed into Trafalgar Square, surged along to Buckingham Palace.

We cheered and waved as Churchill and the King and Queen came out on the balcony, swayed and linked arms with the crowd, swept along with the sheer exuberance of it all. The singing and dancing went on all night and I stayed on, never a thought of Mum and Dad worrying about me at home.

The following weeks were a sort of anticlimax. The war was over for us though we still had troops fighting in the Middle East. The fall of Germany had done nothing to ease their plight – until Japan surrendered, victory would not be complete. After all the rejoicing we still had food shortages and rationing and bleak austerity all around us. Little had changed. It was like the first days of war when the momentous news had made little impact on life for the ordinary citizen.

In July 1945, Dad booked a holiday for us all at a guest house in Sandown, Isle of Wight. No self-catering, Mum was going to have meals cooked for her and be waited on. I think he hoped to recreate our holiday six years ago in August 1939 which had been so disastrously shattered. But somehow the Isle of Wight holiday was not a great success.

My sister Dorothy and I were now fifteen and eighteen respectively and much had happened to us in the intervening years. Mum was worn out and tired. Dad himself was in poor health, edgy and irritable while my brother John, eight, played up and misbehaved the whole time.

While we were in the Isle of Wight the general election was held on 26 July, giving the Labour Party a landslide victory. Churchill resigned as leader of the Conservative Party and Clement Attlee became prime minister.

Dad could not believe it; he was a fervent Tory supporter and Churchill was his idol. To have his hero defeated after winning the war for us – in Dad's eyes – was a bitter blow and the last straw at the end of a not very happy holiday.

On 6 August the atom bomb was dropped on Hiroshima, followed later by another one on Nagasaki. On 15 August 1945 Japan surrendered and the war was finally over.

## POTSDAM

Few, including those in the armed forces, had the remotest idea about the US strategy to use nuclear weapons on Japan in order to end the war. Indeed, very few scientists had really understood the shattering significance of using atomic power. For behind that unexpected change of Britain's prime minister following the UK general election at the end of July lay another dramatic event. It took place in Germany in the days from 17 July to 2 August.

The Potsdam Conference, as it was known, was set up as a meeting between the 'The Big Three' Allied powers with heads of state Harry S Truman, Joseph Stalin and Winston Churchill.

At this meeting it was hoped that the issues of the international situation post-war would be resolved. Instead, the meeting proved to be something less than satisfactory, as had the previous 'Big Three' Conference at Yalta in February 1945. Each of the three had quite different agendas.

At Potsdam, Stalin was initially unwilling to negotiate the future of those Eastern European countries that were then occupied by Soviet forces. In due course, that negotiation would lead to huge parts of Europe remaining more or less under Soviet control until 1991.

Churchill was on edge about the election news at home. He had to leave the conference midway on 26 July for the result. Just a few days later, his place at Potsdam was taken by the new British prime minister, Clement Attlee.

Truman had the heaviest secret of all. In April, the US president, Franklin D Roosevelt, had died, ending World War II's important relationship between Roosevelt and Churchill. As the new US president – he had been Roosevelt's vice president – Truman was about to sign off on the use of the atomic bomb on Japan's Hiroshima and Nagasaki. This would bring the war finally to its close.

Truman did not know that by then Stalin was already developing the Soviet nuclear agenda, and they were already in the process of making their own atomic weapons.

But he did reveal – to Churchill only – that the US had successfully tested the atom bomb. This came as a relief to Churchill given his feelings about Stalin, knowing him to be a brutal tyrant. (Later he would reveal to his doctor, Lord Moran: 'If the Russians had got it, it would have been the end of civilisation.') So it was a suspicious and uneasy trio that posed for the world's cameras as they sat down together in those final days of the war.

Some agreement was made at Potsdam: demilitarised Germany would be split into four separate occupation zones, overseen by the US, Britain, France and the Soviet Union. Historically, however, this was an end to the British Empire's power – and the beginning of the Soviet-led Cold War which Churchill would publicly declare, before President Truman, in the US in March 1946.

'From Stettin in the Baltic to Trieste in the Adriatic, an Iron Curtain has descended across the Continent,' said Churchill at the time.

* * *

Yet for those children living through the war in Britain, the declaration of the end of war meant just one thing – an enormously exciting celebration.

Eleanor McInery lived with her parents in the London suburb of Bexley in Kent. She was four years old when she and her mother were evacuated for safety. They went to Clitheroe, Lancashire, only to discover that the area faced its own Blitz from 1940 to 1942. So she and her mother returned to Bexley – only to live through the V-1 rocket attacks in the south-east in the autumn of 1944. She recalls:

I was never frightened.

My first wartime memory is helping my mother fill sandbags. She was equipped with the little shovel from the coal scuttle that sat by the fireplace.

There were no seaside holidays that year – the beaches were full of barbed wire and landmines – but never mind, there was sand here at home. I had my bucket and spade, I was in business! I shovelled with a will.

Sadly, none of the sandbags were used to protect our house. It must have been the sound of the bomb falling that woke me, for it landed directly in the house across the road. The first thing I saw as I opened my eyes was the curtains billowing in the blast from the detonation, and the shattered fragments of the window falling into the room like a waterfall.

My parents were revising their decision not to sleep in the public air-raid shelter at the end of the road. They picked me up out of my coat, complete with all my bedding, and headed for the stairs. Our flat was on the first floor and I can still remember the sound of plaster that had fallen from the walls crunching under my parents' feet as they went downstairs. My pram was in the hall and it was a good thing they had brought my mattress along because the pram was full of broken glass blown out of the front door. Opening the door was difficult, partly because the blast had damaged the lock and of course there was more plaster underneath, threatening to jam the door still further.

Once outside, they carried me, my bedding, my pram and assorted bits of broken glass and plaster down the flight of steps to the pavement. The air was full of the booming of anti-aircraft guns. The sky, black except where covered by cloud banks of smoke coloured a dull red by fires everywhere, was criss-crossed by searchlights questing for bombers.

Once into the shelter, I was loaded into one of the bunks that were fixed to the bare brick walls. People were sitting in little groups – friends, families, talking quietly or here and there trying to cheer themselves up by singing the favourite songs of the time. My parents obviously thought I was taking more interest in my surroundings than was good for me, and I was turned firmly back to face the wall. And told to go back to sleep. Not much of a view, so I began to pick at the cement between the bricks with my nails, baby nails, soft as paper. I can still remember the sharp grittiness of the cement cutting into my fingers. Then I drifted off to sleep…

Our house was considered uninhabitable and we were moved to a rest centre, a school bereft of its pupils who had all been evacuated en masse. Here, life got even more interesting. Some big girls took me to the cloakrooms, stood me in front of a mirror and gave me a lipstick to play with. My return to the bosom of my family caused quite a sensation: my parents did not approve of cosmetics and my mother scrubbed my face diligently.

We were surrounded by scores of families all in the same boat: homeless, many with only the clothes they stood up in and having no idea what their futures might be, and all trying to stay cheerful. Keeping cheerful was a sort of patriotic duty. Giving way to sorrow or depression was like letting Hitler get the upper hand – not to be contemplated.

My mother and I were evacuated to Clitheroe in Lancashire, while my father stayed behind in London. He had served in the First World War and had been a regular soldier for many years. He was not too old and disabled to be considered for active service again, but he had joined the Home Guard – he did regular fire-watching from the roof of his factory where he worked.

My mother and I had scarcely arrived at our Lancashire billet before Liverpool was subjected to a particularly fierce bombing raid. Locals regarded us Londoners with deep misgivings; Liverpool had never been bombed like that before we came; obviously the entire Luftwaffe were pursuing us – and just hit Liverpool by mistake!

Eventually the Blitz ran its course and we were able to come back to London where the family reunited. After a while though, the whole 'AIR-RAID WARNING, TAKE COVER, SIT OUT THE RAID, ALL-CLEAR, BACK TO NORMAL' routines started up again. If the sirens started while we were at school

our teachers would troop their classes down to the basement and endeavour to boost our morale by leading us
in community singing like 'Ten Green Bottles' and 'One
Man Went to Mow'.

My parents were spared having to decide not to
choose the communal shelter this time. The council had
built shelters in the backyards of our terrace, one shelter
between every two houses, and at that time each address
housed two families, upstairs and downstairs. There was
a party wall built across the middle of each shelter so
that each house had its own half, but there was a large
aperture in the wall so that we could all communicate
and socialise if we chose. My parents kept contact to a
minimum, but the aperture ensured that we were all well
aware that the other half sat out the raids equipped with
a wireless that ran on accumulator batteries, Thermos
flasks of ready-made tea, sometimes biscuits and a jug
of National Dried Milk (introduced after food rationing
arrived in 1940 and known as 'household milk' since
each tin was said to equal four pints of liquid milk when
water was added). Despite the cramped space there was
music, laughter, chats and even a little dancing!

In our half we sat and listened while the old lady
from downstairs gave us a running commentary on
the progress of each doodlebug. One could hear the
rattle growl as it approached and she would tell us, 'It's
coming, it's coming, it's coming' – then her voice would
grow sepulchral – 'IT'S STOPPED!'

Once the motor had cut out the rocket went into silent freefall and you could count (I think it was five seconds) before you heard the explosion. If you didn't hear the explosion it was because it had already landed on you and 'For you, Tommy, the war was over'.

If all this sounds like an appalling environment for a young girl to be growing up in, I have to say I cannot ever remember feeling frightened. Against a background of food rationing and shortages of everything, I regarded air raids and rocket attacks as a type of extreme bad weather; if it came you took what cover you could, sat it out and eventually it would go away.

All through the war, one lady had made a weekly round, door to door with a collecting tin, 'For the Victory Party, when we win the War'. Now the raiders had all gone, treaties had been signed and prisoners exchanged, it was time to count up the party fund and spend it!

The street party started in bright sunshine and went on until well after dark.

A bonfire was lit, and although my generation had never seen a firework before, someone had produced a celebratory rocket. This, however, was not the sort where you stood the stick in a milk bottle, lit the blue touchpaper and retired immediately.

No, this monster was secured somehow to a lamp post for stability. We were all herded well back on the other side of the road and a long fuse was lit.

The rocket, quivering and hissing, released a stream of sparks and smoke, and finally shook itself free of the lamp post and leapt into the air, dashing higher and higher, above the street, above the school, before exploding, raining bright stars all over us and lighting up the entire area around us. This was no ordinary firework, but some sort of signal rocket. It must have been smuggled home by someone's daddy returning from the Navy.

There was music, there was singing and dancing but soon after the rocket my parents decided it was time I went to bed. I protested but they took me indoors and showed me the kitchen clock.

'See that? That's midnight. Now you know what happened to Cinderella, don't you?'

I stared, fascinated, at the two overlapping vertical hands. A magic time. I went quietly to bed and lay listening to the music on the street below.

The war was definitely over.

In Chippenham, Wiltshire, four-year-old Joan Ratcliff was at school when the news broke that the war was over. Joan's father, Stan, was serving in the RAF in Malta. Joan and her mother, Lily, had previously lived with Joan's grandparents in Chobham, Surrey, but were later evacuated to a house in Chippenham.

The first that Joan knew that something very special had happened was when the head teacher came in and whispered something in her teacher's ear.

Both ladies grabbed each other and did a little dance in front of the blackboard.

The children thought it was ever so funny and everybody laughed.

'Oh my word!' cried the teacher, Mrs Paget. 'We think the war is over − we do think that Germany has surrendered now!' She was crying and both ladies ran out of the classroom together. Suddenly, as an afterthought, Mrs Paget ran back, totally flustered and waving her arms in the air.

'Stay there children, stay there!' she laughed and cried at the same time. 'I'll be back in a minute.'

They all sat in silence, not understanding what was going on at all but too amazed to make a noise or run about. The teacher came back a few minutes later having recovered her composure.

It was, indeed, true. Suddenly there was the sound of squealing from the older children in the next-door classroom. Some were frightened at the sudden activity and started crying while others thought it was great fun to have something different going on.

Then the church bells started. Most of the children had never heard the sound before. They had been stopped before they were born. Everyone ran out into the playground to listen as more church bells joined in as the message spread. Some of the youngsters, many of whom were still little more than three years old, clung to the skirts of any adult they could find.

'Miss' tried once again to compose herself and spoke to the children, tears streaming down her face.

'All of you, go back to your tables!' she cried. 'I am sure your mummies will be coming for you soon. You can go home as soon as they arrive.'

Almost as soon as she had finished speaking, excited people started to arrive at the school to take their children away, as the teachers manfully tried to keep notes of who went where. Not that it mattered – very few would be back.

Joan sat and waited as her friends, one by one, were taken away by their emotional mothers. She tried to colour her pictures but there was so much going on it was hard to concentrate. Then, one of the older girls arrived with some milk and little orange tins of Ovaltine tablets (malted milk tablets used as an energy boost during the war).

But gradually the classroom emptied, and the bells did not stop.

Every so often one of the other teachers ran in and gave Mrs Paget a hug and then did a little dance and ran out again.

The children thought it was all very odd indeed. All they did understand was that everybody seemed to be very happy all of a sudden so it stopped them from being too frightened.

Finally Lily arrived, crying and laughing, temporarily forgetting that there was still a war going on in the Far East. It wasn't yet over for the head teacher Mrs Williams who was sending the children on their way. Her husband was still out there somewhere and she didn't even know where. When it occurred to Lily she tried to show a bit of decorum as she shook hands with Mrs Williams.

'I'm sure it will be all over in the Far East too!' she said. 'And your husband will be home safely!'

Mrs Williams gave her a watery smile.

It was still early afternoon as Joan and her friend Ann walked down the road with their mothers, but this time instead of going back to their house in Palmer Street, everyone seemed to be moving in the general direction of the Market Square. The whole place was packed and people were smiling and singing 'Rule Britannia'.

Some American soldiers drove through the streets in their Army vehicles, honking the horns and with their headlights flashing. Others picked the children up, whirling them and their mothers around in the air.

Lily thought everywhere had gone mad and was grateful when two Canadian soldiers swung their daughters up onto their shoulders out of the way of the trampling feet of the crowds. It was like being in a dream only this time they did not want to wake up. After six years it was hard to take in and she wished so much that Stan was there with them.

Somebody turned up with an accordion and started playing 'Hokey Cokey' and everybody formed a circle and did the dance together with all the children.

Union Jacks appeared out of nowhere, just as if their owners had been in readiness for this very special moment.

Then another person started off 'Hands, Knees and Boomps-a-Daisy' and the children found themselves being put down on the floor again as they bumped their bottoms against the shins of the adults towering above them in their efforts to do the dance.

Above all the continuous sound of cheering and singing could be heard the relentless church bells, gradually being added to by those from neighbouring places of worship as the bell-ringers got into the buildings and dusted them down.

## 'YOU'LL WASH YOUR SKIN AWAY FOR THAT YOUNG MAN'

Joan Blackburn, twenty-one, from Leeds had been seconded to an office in Bath, Somerset, in 1944. Joan's sweetheart, Tommy, had been in a POW camp in Germany for some time. Joan had not seen Tommy for nearly five years. She recounts:

VE Day came when I'd been at the office for just over a year. With some friends from the office, including the boss and his wife, we all rushed down to the centre of Bath and found a nice pub where we had a celebratory meal and lots of drinks.

Later in the evening we joined the crowds dancing around Bath Abbey until the small hours. Someone suggested going to London to celebrate there, so we caught the early morning train with a two-hour journey to Paddington and somehow – tube, taxi, walking, we made our way to St Paul's Cathedral, the symbol of Britain surviving the Blitz. Hundreds of people were walking around.

Knowing I'd always dreamed of working in Fleet Street after the war, we then went straight there, looking at all the great newspaper buildings and ending up at the famous journalists' pub, The Cheshire Cheese. Carried along by euphoria we then walked all the way to Park Lane, talking to strangers all the way. A distant relative with a flat near the Dorchester Hotel took us in for a cup of tea and a wash. We arrived back in Bath in the early hours of the morning.

We had to be back in the office by 8.30am. 'Back to work' said the boss. 'Our war isn't over yet.'

During the morning the phone went. I answered the phone for the boss and it was Tommy wanting to speak to me. After all the celebrations from the office how could I ask the boss for leave? Everyone in the office knew about Tommy and I got permission to go home.

The rent I paid in my digs only allowed me one bath a week and if I wanted another one I had to pay an extra sixpence!

On this occasion the landlord said: 'You'll wash your skin away for that young man' but he allowed me to have a bath. He and his wife had heard all about Tommy and seemed as thrilled as I was.

During the journey from Bath to Leeds, I poured out my excitement to an elderly lady on the train who gently warned me that I should not expect to see the healthy young man I had last seen at Waterloo station in 1940.

Remembering returned prisoners from the First World War, she advised me not to show my shock if Tommy looked pale and thin – and perhaps pot-bellied after a diet of boiled potatoes.

Instead I was met by a sunburnt young man who, having been released by the Americans before the war ended, had spent the previous days marching through Germany and France eating farm food whenever he could, finally reaching England by air in a Dakota – one of the first POWs to arrive in England on VE Day.

In the thrill of our reunion I quite forgot it was I who must have looked pale and tired after the last two days' celebrations in Bath and London without any sleep.

I remember sitting on a fence outside Harewood House near Leeds, thrilled to be together again and then driving back to my family home for a great welcome.

My mother was nearly in tears when she refilled Tom's teacup. He had drained every drop and left only a few tealeaves in the cup.

## 'THIS WAS WHERE GUY HITLER
## MET HIS FATE'

Val Smith was just seven years old on VE Day in Liverpool.

We lived on Smithdown Road. Our road backed on to Penny Lane.

Everyone knew that peace was coming so all the mums in any street planning for a victory party began to save up their rations.

The children could go to the party in fancy dress if they wanted to. I went to dancing class so a couple of my outfits came in useful. My friend Margaret wore my fairy dress and my friend Pat borrowed a maid's outfit.

Another friend called Irene was also a maid; I think her mum made it for her.

I went as Britannia, ruling the waves with a brush handle, cardboard trident and paper shield; my mum made all these things. She took the frills off and the hoops out of one of my dance dresses, but I can't remember how she made the helmet, but with great difficulty I expect.

Mum also made a Hitler guy out of an old suit. He lay in our hall for a couple of weeks and almost became one of the family but he went the same way as all guys (especially one called Hitler), up in smoke to the sound of loud cheering.

On the day of the party the tables were brought out and placed in the road; no bother from cars in those days. You had to be well off to own a car and that didn't apply to us. Then the tablecloths were laid and lastly the food was brought out: sandwiches and jellies and then Mrs Armstrong, the organiser of the party, carried out some fairy cakes and, wonder of wonders, as well as icing on the top each cake had a silver ball on it. Well, that was it, mad panic then. We children had been standing watching all this going on but we still didn't have our chairs. I flew into the house.

'Quick, quick, can I have my chair now, there are cakes on the table with silver balls on!' I had a fear that I would be sitting on the other end of the table from those cakes but panic over, there were enough for us all. Mrs Armstrong had kept those silver balls for just such an event as this. As soon as we were told that we could begin eating, Mum said that every child's hand shot out to that plate of cakes. We weren't sure at first whether we could eat them or not – and had to be told that we could.

We had our bonfires on one side of the road that had been hit by a bomb and we had our bonfires there for years, the VE party being the first.

This is where Guy Hitler met his fate. We stayed up late that night, enjoying an evening round the fire. Finally roasting potatoes in the embers, fishing them out with sticks and having a good tuck in again.

## EVEN IF IT WAS A DIRTY CRACKED EGG
## THEY DIDN'T MIND

Londoner Kathleen Wilson had moved with her family to Brighton, Sussex, in 1938. When war broke out, Kathleen, then fourteen, started working in a grocery store. She carried on working there throughout the war.

8 May 1945, how jubilant we all were. There was so much celebrating. All one could think of was no more bombs, and a little prematurely, I'm afraid, a lot more freedom. We were still at war in the Far East with Japan, but for this moment, we pushed that thought to the back of our minds. Uppermost was victory over Germany.

There was so much happiness and relief – people suddenly seemed to be laughing at nothing. A weight had been lifted from everyone's shoulders.

I begged the boss to let us decorate our provisions window out with red, white and blue crepe paper and it was graciously given. Street parties sprang up everywhere. Food was willingly given for these special celebrations. It was a miracle where it all came from – people must have had food stored up for this very occasion. However, if anyone was misguided enough to think food rationing was going to cease now, they were sadly disappointed. It went on for years.

The next few months was a busy time with the repatriation of many prisoners of war. Brighton held a fair number of them as they passed in transit.

Then came 15 August 1945, VJ Day. The Americans had dropped their atomic bombs on Japan a few days earlier and Japan surrendered unconditionally. Now the war was well and truly over and the celebrations started all over again, but this time they were intensified. We opened our arms to receive the good things we all felt sure would follow. There were more street parties and dancing and bonfires, since there were no blackout restrictions now. There were the sad and bereaved families of course, and we all commiserated with them, but we could not bring people back.

The way ahead was forward and, we hoped, it was a brighter future.

It was not until years afterwards that anyone realised what awful consequences followed the dropping of those bombs on Hiroshima and Nagasaki. Those who survived it were a lot worse off than those who were killed. The ones left behind suffered horrific diseases caused by the intense radiation they received.

With the ending of the war you could say there was an anticlimax because no matter what anyone expected to happen, nothing major changed. Life went on as usual. There were one or two subtle changes but nothing that made any real difference.

At work, I continued to train the apprentices, and often we had two lads at the same time. One would be working out his first year on the grocery counter and the other one would be training with me. The idea of keeping a happy balance in the shop was to keep them apart as much as possible. This was not easy in a small shop.

They enjoyed learning to master the skills of skinning a cheese and cutting up a side of bacon, mainly because these jobs were carried out in the cellar where they were not under scrutiny all the time. None of the apprentices ever took kindly to scrubbing down the woodwork until it dried nearly white, but this job was done once a week because it was essential for hygienic reasons.

We would often find cracked eggs which you could not give out as a customer's allocated ration. People were only allowed one egg a week so there was obviously a great demand for the cracked ones, no matter how badly they were damaged.

Some customers came in with a basin, in the hopes of salvaging an egg that had departed its shell and was residing in the egg tray. Even when there was a little bit of dirt in it they did not mind. Only expectant mothers and young children were allowed three eggs a week and you knew these by their different coloured ration books.

Some of the ration books were in an absolutely disgusting condition. You would look at them with repugnance and not want to handle them. We had one such customer, Mrs Bone, who came into the shop every week with a fox fur round her shoulders and a cat draped cosily round her neck on top of it. I think it was a tabby.

She presented her book without the bat of an eyelid. It looked for all the world as though it had fallen into the frying pan, and besides making you shudder when you touched it, it was almost impossible to delete with a marker. If any of the lads were forced to serve her they would make a song and dance about it, treating the book as if it were contaminated with the plague. One even audaciously asked if anyone had any gloves he could use! Thankfully the boss, Molly Mitchell, never heard him.

The woman just stared stolidly ahead and ignored him completely.

## 'WE STOPPED THEM FROM PUSHING A SPITFIRE INTO THE BONFIRE'

Joe Roddis (1921–2017) was an RAF engine fitter. He had worked on Spitfires during the Battle of Britain and went on to see a great deal of wartime action. On 8 May, when news of the ceasefire came through, Joe was based with 485 Squadron in Germany.

To celebrate, we had a football match. I ran into a barbed wire during the game, put my arm up to save myself and ended up with a bandaged arm!

The fact that the war in Europe had ended didn't seem to sink in immediately but by the end of the day, with all work stopped, the celebrations began. Free booze and food and the mood was set. One rigger had been saving a bottle of Benedictine for this day and he soon polished it off, even though I'd never known him to drink before this day. As the evening wore on, things began to get a bit hectic. Bonfires were lit at the dispersal and when somebody discovered a store filled with artillery shell cases and their contents, they threw them on the fires and things got really hot!

I remember at one stage a crowd of us stopping some lads from pushing a Spitfire into one of the bonfires and that really closed down the celebrations. After that, it was little groups of men just standing around and just drinking quietly, wondering what would happen to us now?

In July, Joe decided to marry Mary, a girl he had met at an Army dance in Emsworth, Hampshire.

On 14 July, the pair tied the knot.

The custom on the squadron when anyone got married was to make a collection and for me the chaps threw in that many marks, francs and Dutch guilders that I could have hired Westminster Abbey for the wedding. Unfortunately you were only allowed to exchange so much of the funny money (Forces notes) for £1 postal orders, but the commanding officer made the exception and changed me £100 which was a fair old sum in those days. There was enough left over for the biggest piss-up we had ever had. Afterwards I entered my bunk and found that the squadron cartoonist 'Ticker' Booth had covered one wall with a life-size chalk drawing, in colour, depicting the wedding ceremony. It was magnificent. I always regretted not getting a photo of it.'

## 'A TERRIBLE SIGHT GREETED ME'

Terry Spencer (1918–2009) joined the RAF in 1941 and started flying Spitfires in 1943. He had a highly eventful flying career throughout the war, ending with a DFC and a Belgian Croix de Guerre avec Palme. After the war Terry worked all over the world as a successful photo journalist for *Life* magazine and the *New York Times*. Yet in those final days of the war, he found himself visiting the infamous concentration camp, Bergen-Belsen, just days after the British forces had liberated the camp on 15 April.

We had no idea of the absolute horror awaiting us there. The sickly smell of lime and death permeated the air from well outside the barbed wire. A terrible sight greeted me. At the entrance to the camp the skeletal frame of a woman had come to greet her liberators and slumped onto the wire, gashing her neck in the process. She was dead.

What I saw there was so horrific I left the camp feeling as if I had had a most terrible nightmare.

Afterwards I talked to Germans who knew about concentration camps but I do not believe any of them knew of the horrors of what had taken place in the camps.

The thought (to me) of resuming a normal, tranquil life was appalling. The war had germinated in me a desire for adventure. Perhaps I also felt I was living on borrowed time and had already become a fatalist. I did not realise it then but my RAF experience was excellent training for photo journalism. It gave me quick reactions, taught me survival and the discipline to go one way towards trouble when the temptation was to do the opposite. Over the years to come I was prepared to take risks to get pictures but only if there was a strong chance of success.

For the final post-war months until my demob at Christmas, I was stationed in Germany. We lived the life of wealthy playboys. We had yachts, horses and Mercedes-Benz cars. There was a lavish country club at nearby Travemünde and though we were banned from fraternising with German girls, they soon became 'Austrian'. We commandeered an eighty-foot torpedo recovery boat. This had a large afterdeck where we danced the nights through with lovely ENSA girls from Lübeck who were there to entertain the troops. Entertainments National Service Association was set up in 1939 to provide entertainment for the armed forces and I was put in charge of wine stores in the area so we were never short of liquor.

My demob came through at Christmas 1945. I felt there must be a market for travel stories after the British people had been cooped up on their small island for six years, virtually cut off from the outside world. Severe rationing had become a way of life. They were tired and dreary. Perhaps I could show them another life, so here I was, on my way to the unknown.

# CHAPTER 2

# IT'S OVER
## ... ISN'T IT?

*'Our peace shall stand as rocky mountains'*
WILLIAM SHAKESPEARE, *HENRY V, PART II*

In those months after VE Day, the election surprise and the ncws of Japan's H-bomb devastation, there was a surge of sheer escapism. The shops, of course, could not provide much that was cheerful to buy. The many shortages remained in place. Yet the familiar wartime entertainments were always available for the price of a few pence.

Cinemas were packed out – the movie *Brief Encounter* (still around today) was launched to crowded audiences in November 1945, a romantic love story doomed never to reach fulfilment viewed now as a historical emblem of typical 1940s middle-class lives – with a reminder of quiet, restrained, British stoicism.

Interestingly, the star of *Brief Encounter*, the actress Celia Johnson (1908–82), was filming *Brief Encounter* at Denham Studios, Buckinghamshire, at the same time as the news of VE Day was due to be announced.

As the victory day drew near, the atmosphere in the studio got more excited. A few days before, Johnson had written to her husband, Peter Fleming, who was in India.

'Victory gets nearer and nearer,' she wrote. Her plan for VE Day, she said, was to light a bonfire for the children (her two sons at home in Oxfordshire).

In fact, Celia Johnson went home and did just that, helping to light a village bonfire with four repatriated prisoners of war. 'It was a beautiful night,' she wrote.

Churchill had frequently understood the value of the huge wartime cinema audiences when it came to boosting morale. In 1944, a hugely popular movie of Shakespeare's *Henry V* had been released in colour, coinciding with the Normandy landings and the Allied advance into France. Churchill had, in fact, instructed the movie's star and director, Sir Laurence Olivier, to fashion the movie as a morale booster for the troops – highly successful propaganda for audiences, entertainment as spin, as it were.

Dance halls across the country were equally crowded after VE Day. For the moment, at least, people were determined to relax a little, dance, laugh and appreciate what was now a huge relief.

Upheaval, however, remained a constant thread as everywhere across the country families were gradually uprooted, returning to the homes they'd left behind.

The return started in late 1944. Once again, as in September 1939 when war broke out, groups of evacuated children pinned to labels and carrying suitcases climbed on to trains to bring them home.

By April 1945, the Ministry of Health laid out plans for the return of half a million London evacuees including schoolchildren, mothers, babies, the elderly and the disabled. These were due to be returned by special trains. Parents had the option to request free travel vouchers to collect their children.

The following month, all London schools were closed for one week. This allowed teachers to discover more about the conditions the returning children might find. The children's labels were either marked HOME, i.e. they could return, or NO HOME, meaning the children faced returning to bombed-out homes perhaps with family members still living in bombed-out accommodation that was unacceptable for the young.

In some instances, one or both parents might have been killed – or the parents of evacuees might not now be willing to care for their children.

In many cases, the children had to remain in reception areas until their accommodation could be organised. By August 1945, over 70,000 children were still living in reception areas – thanks mostly to severe housing problems in the devastated cities.

Orphaned children were often evacuated to the country and then returned to a family member, happy to house the orphaned child back to the area they'd first lived in.

## 'I WAS TOLD THEY'D TAKEN ME OUT SHOPPING AND LOST ME'

Ellen Steel was a five-year-old, living with her parents and baby brother in a block of flats called Hilton House on the Honor Oak Estate in Brockley, south-east London. In March 1941, during the Blitz, Ellen and her family were seeking shelter in the laundry room of Hilton House when the building received a direct hit.

I was in hospital for three days but all I had was a cut on my head and bruises on my body. I was told many years later when I was twenty-one that a policeman who lived in Hilton House was on night duty that evening. Hearing that the block had had a direct hit, he came to search for his wife and little girl, who was six years old.

He found me and he was the one that took me to safety. But sadly his wife and daughter had been killed – along with my parents and baby brother. My mother was identified by my aunt by a scar on her right hand. My baby brother, Raymond, was laid beside Mum in the same coffin.

All that was left of my parents was a purse and a wallet containing my dad's driving licence. In the purse was a receipt – Mum was paying off for a little dress for me, green and white, costing twenty-four shillings (roughly £38 today). My Aunt Nance got the dress for me and I had my photo done in it. I still have it.

When I came out of hospital I went to live briefly with my Aunt Nance and Uncle Thomas and their two children, Gladys and Bob. Then I was evacuated to a farm in Devon.

I kept asking for my mum and dad but my aunt and uncle never told me my parents and brother had been killed. I remember believing that they had just taken me out shopping and lost me. In those days they did not talk about such things as death to children, and I never had the sense to put two and two together.

I stayed on a farm in Devon for a year. For a whole year there were no air-raid warnings or bombs dropping so I had no fear. After a year my Uncle Thomas collected me and brought me home to London. So I went back to live with them and their children in their two-bed-room railway house in Brockley. My uncle worked for the railways.

When an air-raid warning came we had to run out of the house along the road to the shelter beneath the railway arches, which we shared with another family. During night-time air raids we'd sleep in the shelter until the all-clear went. If it was a day raid we would play cards and sing; my favourite was 'Run Rabbit Run'. If the raid went on for hours then my aunt, if she wasn't working, would go home and cook us a meal quickly, something like powdered mash and Spam [canned cooked pork, very popular in World War II].

I also remember the day I was playing with other children in my road when a boy called Peter said in a loud voice, 'Your mum and dad are dead'.

I went in crying to my aunt and told her what he had said – that was how I found out that my parents and brother had been killed.

During the war my aunt got thirteen shillings a week for looking after me (equivalent to £25 today). A lady from the Ministry of Pensions would come to check on me now and again, and I was always afraid she would take me away. On one of her visits she asked my aunt if I would like to live in Canada, as there were children being shipped out there.

My aunt said to me, in front of the lady, 'Well, would you like to go?'

Of course I said no. The last visit from the lady came just before I left school in 1949. I had to meet her outside the post office with my savings book and she put a small amount of money in it for my start in life. I had no more contact with her because I was about to leave school.

After the war, people who had lost everything in the bombing were paid 'War Damage' money. My aunt had to apply for it and as the only survivor, the money came to me – £112.00 (around £3,500 today).

I dearly wanted a bike as I had never had one of my own. My aunt let me spend £12 on a brand-new bike, bought from a shop in Lewisham. The remaining £100 went into my post office savings.

As a war orphan, the Salvation Army were always very kind to me, and gave me clothes once a year. I would also receive an annual parcel from Canada: tiny little gifts and a slice of fruit cake, but the best thing was a little white hair slide with coloured flowers on it. I used to wear it a lot, I thought it was so beautiful.

The Mayor of Deptford gave a party for war orphans and children who'd lost their fathers in action. It was held in New Cross Town Hall.

War orphans were not forgotten. Years later when I was nineteen and about to be married, Marshal Tito from Yugoslavia came to Britain in 1953 and left a large sum of money to be shared amongst war orphans. It was advertised in the newspaper so I applied. A lady came to interview me and then she wrote to me several weeks later to say she was so sorry but I was not entitled to any money because I had all my limbs. She said to try again but I never did. I borrowed my wedding dress and veil and married the man I loved.

There were other children who had been evacuated to rural, more pleasant surroundings, yet were very unhappy with the return back to their old life. Some were very attached to the families who had taken them in and had given them a very different, often healthier way of life in the country. Others might have left the city with their own family and embraced the very different environment they had found themselves in.

## 'I CRIED FOR AGES WHEN WE GOT BACK.'

Ten-year-old Doris Grimsley wasn't in the least bit happy when her family eventually returned to London.

At four and a half years of age, the declaration of war didn't mean much to me.

We lived in a small terraced house in Plumstead, south-east London, where we'd moved from the East End with my parents and grandmother. The Matchless Motor Cycle factory was in our road and the big Woolwich Arsenal munitions factory was very near, so my parents were fearful of air raids. [Matchless motor bikes were highly popular until the mid-1960s.]

I had started school briefly in May 1940 and my sister was born in July that year. By the time I should have returned to school after the summer break, London was badly bombed. So my mother took me and my baby sister to stay with a family in Peterborough in Northamptonshire.

We were only there for a month because my father had a transfer from his job at the Woolwich Arsenal to a new armaments factory in Risley, Lancashire. We were to be given a council house to rent in Haydock, seven miles away from Risley, and so we moved from London just before Christmas. We moved into our house early in January. There was about six feet of snow up the door and it was very cold.

The house was in a small estate built for the workers at the factory and we were a mixed bunch but there were lots of other children around to play with. A nice mixed-race girl called Helen lived opposite, and another friend was Eunice Markoff, daughter of Jewish parents. The few toys we had we shared – a skate, a few marbles, a doll's pram, a few home-made dolls and some old tennis balls. Also mother's long clothes line was stretched across the road, we took it in turns to turn the rope while about six of us skipped in line.

We also chalked hopscotch on the pavement and played that game with a stone; we'd play for hours. We also had French knitting, when we could get some scraps of wool. The only time we knew there was a war on was at night when the planes went over to bomb Liverpool. Of course, we all gathered around the small Bakelite radio to hear the news. What Churchill was telling us seemed to comfort the grown-ups.

I went to a church school about a mile from where we lived. It was near a colliery so on our walks to and from school we'd pass the miners' cottages and see the men coming off shift covered in coal. When we were older we played on the slag heaps, getting filthy.

Occasionally on the walk home from school one of the boys who had a penknife would cut a turnip from a farmer's field, wipe the dirt off on his trousers and cut it into thin slices; that would give us enough energy to get home.

I only had one sweet during the whole of the war and that was a piece of nougat when the local shop had some in. Other than that we had liquorice root to chew or some cocoa powder mixed with a bit of sugar and put into the bottom of a newspaper cone, you could lick a finger and dip it into the mixture to make it last all the way to school.

School was nice when I was in the infants. We had a little nap in the afternoons when all the tables were turned upside down and cushions put in them for us to lie in. It was lovely. When I went up to the juniors it wasn't so lovely, as the teachers were very strict and I frequently got rapped over the knuckles with a ruler.

I made friends with two local girls, Audrey Dale and Cora Kay. I had to speak 'Lancashire' when I was with my friends and 'south London' when I was at home. If I was out with my parents and run into my friends I was struck dumb!

We weren't affected by the bombing but we felt the effects of food and clothes rationing. We had our own chickens, and it was my job to collect the eggs. But if we had more than six a day we had to pass them on elsewhere. We also grew our own vegetables. One day I fell over a potato sack and cut my leg. There was no money to pay for a doctor and, of course, no NHS at that time. So my mother put the odd sixpence in a pot on the mantelpiece to pay for any emergency doctor's treatment we might need. Dad seemed to know the right people.

Sometimes he brought a piece of meat home and said he'd got it on the black market.

On Sunday evenings we spent our time cutting up newspapers into squares, making a hole in the corner and threading a bundle of them onto string for use in the lavatory. Toilet paper was unavailable.

The local Picturedrome drew us like magnets, with Roy Rogers and Trigger or the Three Stooges comedies. We children sat on forms in front for threepence each. The miners' wives sat behind in the sixpenny seats and they brought bags of peas with them to shell for their husbands' meals. If we were lucky they'd give us some peas to keep us quiet.

The coat I had for most of the war was a grey astra-khan made by my mother out of one of her coats. It had a hood and mittens fastened on with elastic. It was big for me when I was six but like a blazer when I got to ten. Most things to wear were home-made except vests, liberty bodices, knickers and black wool stockings which came from the local haberdashers and were handed down from family to family. Even hair ribbon was on coupons, so woe betide me if I lost one! Our clothes were worn for a week, vest and knickers kept on for bed, so they needed a good boil-up in the copper.

We remained in Haydock on VE Day, 8 May, and Dad then had a choice of moving to another factory further north or taking his chances of getting a job back in London.

As both my parents were Londoners from the East End they decided to return but it was February 1946 before we came back.

Gran had kept up the rent on our small house so we moved back in with her, but it was very cramped.

I cried for ages when we got back, thinking my parents would allow me to go back to Haydock when they saw how unhappy I was. But no such luck.

I was back in London for good and nothing prepared me for the sight of the shabby buildings, bomb sites and lack of trees and grass. When I went to school, the other children were a few years behind me in education.

It wasn't until years later that I realised how fortunate I had been as 'my war' was vastly different to that experienced in the south – and many cities in the British Isles.

## 'I WAS ACCUSTOMED TO BEING IN THE WAR'

Karen Steele was born in 1935. She and her younger sister, Barbara, lived in Ilford, just outside London with their mother, Ruby. Her father, Syd, was in the armed forces abroad. The family went through some of the worst of the southern wartime bombings. (Ilford suffered hundreds of high explosive bombs through the war as well as the V-1s and V-2s towards the end of the war.)

My mum must have been petrified about what might happen to us.

Ilford was near the docks. Bombs were often being dropped over Ilford almost every night.

Mum would have been sitting there thinking, 'When is it our turn?'

Barbara is much younger than me and we'd huddle together in the Anderson shelter; yet as a child you somehow accept it all. The morning after each bomb, the kids in our street would be out there on the wrecked houses, looking for shrapnel. Because you were more or less born into it, that didn't seem unusual. The whole thing was part of your life.

I was very excited on VE Day, though it wasn't because we knew the war was officially over. I was going up to London on the train with my favourite aunt, Sylvia, my dad's sister, who worked in Downing Street. She often visited us.

She'd booked us tickets for the theatre which to me was wonderful; Sylvia always spoiled me rotten. She'd take me on outings, bring me presents, that sort of thing.

The odd thing was, neither of us understood we were about to be right in the very centre of the London celebrations for VE Day. We just came up the stairs out of Piccadilly underground and there it all was, people all over the place, shouting, singing, perched on Eros, linking arms and dancing, like being in the middle of a mad circus, all so exciting for a child. All the lights of Piccadilly were blazing – a novelty in itself because we'd just ended the blackouts and all the darkness.

We managed to make our way up Shaftesbury Avenue into the Lyric Theatre, more swarms of people, some dressed up, all smiling, laughing; the atmosphere was incredible.

The play was *Duet for Two Hands* starring John Mills and his new wife, Mary Hayley Bell. At the end John Mills came out and made a Victory speech, and of course everyone clapped and cheered like mad. It was all so thrilling, a ten-year-old going to a big theatre at night with my favourite aunt in the middle of all this joy and celebration. By the time we got back to Ilford I went to sleep thinking I'd had the best day ever.

I was so accustomed to life being a child during the war, I remember afterwards saying to my mother: 'Mummy, what's going to go on the news now the war is over?' That's how it was: all we'd ever heard about on the radio was the war.

The other odd thing about it all was my dad was away in the Army but when he came back, I didn't know, for some reason, exactly what he'd been doing – and I didn't discover the truth until many years later when he was elderly.

It turned out he'd been working in bomb disposal.

'Best job in the Army' he told me. 'Everyone loved us. Wherever you went, everything was on the house for the bomb disposal guys.

The homecoming was a different story for each one of the four million British servicemen who were officially demobilised between June 1945 and January 1947. Joan Blackburn here writes about her grandfather, Stan:

## 'IT WAS GROUND HITLER NEVER GOT TO WALK ON – THOUGH HE CAME MIGHTY CLOSE'

Stan Ratcliff tried to keep on his feet amongst the crowd of men all trying to be the first to see the coast of England again. If any more of them tried to push towards the front of the little minesweeper carrying them it would surely turn turtle.

His tour of duty for the RAF in Egypt was over. It had been a long and tiring journey from Egypt to Palestine and then along the North African coast. The men slept on tables in the canteen and on any spare piece of floor there was, along with the crew, and all with one aim in common – to get back home as quickly as possible by whatever method!

He had written to the folks and his wife Lily but they didn't know exactly when to expect him, any more than he did. All he could do was phone neighbour Mr Gabriel when the ship arrived at Portsmouth. It was already three months since VE Day and the mail had been all over the place.

'Now, there's a situation!' he thought to himself. 'I bet the queue for the phones will be a mile long – I could simply get on the train and get home quicker than it would take to let them know.'

The ship was rocking about and it was all he could do to stay upright but it was a mix of adrenaline and euphoria that was keeping everyone going. Nervousness too – most of the men had not seen their loved ones for years and didn't know what they would find when they got home.

'You OK, Flight?'

He couldn't complain about his promotion. He had arrived in Malta a corporal and left as a sergeant and now, on leaving Egypt, he was a flight sergeant.

He turned round and saw the familiar face of his second in command from the MT (Motor Transport) Section, corporal 'Chalky White'.

'God Almighty, I'll be glad to get off this boat won't you, Flight?' he growled.

'Even having a pee is a major operation – damn it, I've just been over the side – it's not exactly the latest in luxury, is it?'

Stan laughed. 'Well at least we are in one piece, corporal – I feel as though I have used up all of my nine lives a hundred times over and, frankly, I couldn't care less if it was a tin bath!'

The pushing and shoving carried on as the ship waited to dock, amongst dozens of others of various shapes and sizes. A brass band was playing on the quayside and people were waving Union Jacks. It was just one great wall of sound and many of the men had tear-stained faces. Most of them had been seasick, but the awful journey was forgotten in the elation of being home.

The friends hung onto their kitbags and waited patiently as the minesweeper docked.

'Keep well, Chalky!' Stan patted him on the back, 'Who knows, maybe our paths will cross again.'

The two men hugged each other and then Stan turned round to thank some of the crew. They had put up with so much on the journey back. All would have tales to tell and all had mixed feelings ranging between hysteria, elation, sadness and the horrors of war.

He could see now why his father never spoke about the First World War. It wasn't the sort of thing you could speak about. It was like the old man had said: 'You could speak about the going and you could speak about the coming back – it was the bit in between that you would rather draw a veil over.'

The only thing any of the blokes had on their mind just at this moment in time was to get home and Stan had already missed his daughter's fourth birthday by a long way.

He felt in his uniform pocket and pulled out a screwed-up photo of Lily with his daughter Joan. His wife looked as beautiful as ever with her slim figure and dark curls and the youngster was no longer a baby, but a little girl.

A wave of bitterness swept over him at missing out on most of his child's babyhood, followed almost immediately by guilt. There were so many around him straining for a glimpse of a loved one, or rushing for the first train to where they were. At least his journey was almost over.

Stan was pushed along with the flow of humanity, and he slung his kitbag onto his shoulder. His feet were on English soil and for many of the younger men the emotion became too much.

It was all over – for most of them so was life in the military and there would be a lot of adjusting to do. He felt like kissing the ground and many around him did. It was ground that Hitler would never get to walk on after all, though he came mighty close.

## 'THE POSH GIT FROM NORTON GREEN'

For the young, the end of war meant the dawn of a new life at work.

Frank Mee was born in 1929 in Norton, a small village in Stockton-on-Tees. His father was a haulage contractor, his mother a dressmaker and tailoress. Frank, his sister, Sylvia, and their parents lived in a three-bedroom house with a walled garden and a smallholding with brick stables.

Dad was also a gardener supreme, so we lived off our own produce, with ducks, pigs, geese, hens and even goats. Fruit and vegetables were preserved or stored.

My aunt and uncle had a dairy farm just up the road, making their own butter and cream. Wartime shortages were never a problem, as people in our part of the world were mainly self-sufficient.

My mother had ambitions for me to rise in the world like my Uncle Raymond, the youngest boy in Middlesbrough (at the time) to get a Higher National Certificate (a higher education qualification).

Lots of my friends never made it to high school, mostly because many families could not afford uniforms and the books and kit you had to have. I made it to leaving school at nearly sixteen, the best we could expect at the time. University was way above our heads. Most kids left school at twelve or thirteen, a few making it to the then school-leaving age of fourteen.

In November 1944 I finished my exams. I was still fifteen. I spent a lot of time reading up engineering books: I knew what I wanted to do. My mother wanted me to go to Durham Agricultural College to be a gentleman farmer but no way, I thought, I knew farming, it was 24/7 – with no holidays! The main engineering firms locally sent out letters of introduction to the school, asking them to send boys from engineering classes for interviews.

So I was asked to accompany one of my classmates, John Hunton, on an interview to Browns Sheet Iron Works in Stockton. The interview was for an apprentice.

We went into an office on the ground floor with windows looking out on what seemed, to me, to be utter chaos akin to Dante's *Inferno*, sparks flying, machines crashing metal, men hitting things with hammers.

'Good grief!' I thought, 'Who would work in that?'

John was given a couple of problems to solve by the man interviewing us while I gazed out at what I'd then have described as Hell. John had always been slow at maths and he failed the test problems but he was offered a job in the wire works. He wound up working there for the rest of his life and retiring as manager for the wire products.

Then it was my turn. I was asked to do a test on paperwork. Technical drawing was my top skill so that was easy.

'Right, start Monday. The day you turn sixteen you become an apprentice.'

'No way,' was my response. 'Have a look outside, talk to some of the men,' I was told. I opened the door and then I heard something strange. It was the men, singing to music. Speakers were on the wall.

I thought: 'If they're all singing, it can't be so bad.'

At home there was a big argument with my mother. 'Go down and look for yourself, Gladys, my dad said. 'Then decide.'

Sometime later, my parents walked back into the house, laughing. They all knew each other at the firm from the dancing competitions they always attended.

So I started work on the Monday…

It had been an eye-opening adventure for me, starting work. A six-day week, Saturday a normal working day, my evenings were night school and two nights dancing. On Sunday nothing opened, not even the cinema. Sunday lunch was visits from the family and sitting round the piano playing or Uncle Peter playing when we all sang.

'The posh git from Norton Green,' as they called me, found himself landing amongst lads who had been working from ages twelve or thirteen, so I had to prove myself – which at one stage meant bare knuckle fists, the entertainment for the works in the lunch breaks.

Insults would fly until I was provoked into fighting which we could not do on the working floors, so at midday they all carried sandwiches and cans of tea to the top floor which was cleared for marking out large jobs.

A circle was formed as they all chewed on their food and the combatants were pushed into the ring with a second, mine was Steve Small, a quiet married man, whom few ever crossed. One of the best tradesmen in the place.

The works bookie would be shouting the odds. So I knew I was not going to be the winner. My dad had enrolled me in boxing classes when I was ten and I had boxed at school where my claim to fame was knocking the PT teacher on his back, whereupon he got up and beat me up, in a technical way, of course.

There were four fights, three wins and one draw when someone shouted, 'All bets off, it's a draw now, back to work!'

The last one I fought had boasted about what he would do to me, then he mentioned my sister – he went down fast, me onto him and then he was dragged off.

So I had my respect; no more fights to entertain the lunch group.

Across the road from the works was a grocery warehouse. They packed tea which arrived in tea chests and then was blended and packed by girls around my own age.

I fell for one of them. Kitty was fun, beautiful to me, and she agreed to go dancing with me. Problem was, she was Catholic, I was C of E and in those days, never the twain shall meet. So I was never allowed to take her home, dancing was about it.

The dancing went on for quite a few weeks, then she disappeared. I asked where she was and the girls she worked with just said she'd gone away. My work was definitely suffering when Charley, an ex-soldier, took me aside and told me the truth.

Kitty had met an airman at a dance one night. Things had got out of hand and she fell pregnant. As a Catholic girl, she had been taken to a place in the Lake District run by nuns until she had the baby, which was then taken off her at birth and she never saw again.

Sometime later she had come back and I saw her walking down the street and dashed over.

I did not recognise her. Her eyes were dead. She had aged, she looked grey, no smile, she just looked at me and said, 'You do not want to know me, go away,' and she walked on.

I just stood there. Your first-ever heartbreak at sixteen is definitely the worst.

Youngsters like Frank Mee weren't merely experiencing first love on the dance floor in 1945. There were other post-war behaviours in society that continued very much as they had during wartime. The black market, for instance, had been an established response to rationing where goods were sold illegally, 'under the counter', especially cigarettes and alcohol which had not been rationed but were always in short supply.

Purveyors of the black market were known as 'spivs', a slang word describing petty criminals, often sporting a coat with wide lapels, padded shoulders, hair parted in the middle and with a pencil-thin moustache, usually found in the larger cities. The spivs continued their illegal trade beyond the post-war celebrations, as we'll touch on more in the next chapter.

## 'WE WERE ALL SPIVS IN OUR OWN WAY'

'After VE Day, it was two days off and then we were brought back to earth with the boss shouting, "OK, the bloody war's not over yet, get cracking!"

Around the world, fighting was still going on in many places. In Trieste, the Yugoslavs wanted a bit of Italy, and our troops were there to stop them. In Greece we were in a full-scale war as Communist insurgents tried to take over the country. We had occupation troops in Germany and Austria who had to guard small towns and villages, who had not seen much of the war but were suddenly being attacked as thousands of displaced people tried to walk home. Palestine was in turmoil, whilst Egypt, Iran and Iraq had British garrisons to keep the peace. India had riots as they wanted independence.

The war was "over" – but it was not over for many.

It came to an end with Japan unexpectedly. We all thought it was going to be a long time before the Japanese caved in. There was talk of not invading Japan itself but of a blockade and then starving them into submission. It was claimed that about a million troops would die if we invaded. Then came the news of Hiroshima on 6 August, and three days later Nagasaki. Japan surrendered to the allies on 15 August and signed the peace treaty in Tokyo Bay on 2 September. That was the start of people returning back from the Japanese prison camps – and the anger of the population at what had been done to them there.

The war was over but "forget it, get on with life" was the prevailing attitude – while nothing much changed.

We had a new government: Labour by a massive majority, but we young ones thought it was disgusting that the public had cast our hero Winston Churchill aside. He had won the war for us – that was the way we thought about it – and who on earth were these dull men in suits who said they would lead us out of austerity? We did not believe a word of it, but obviously our elders did.

Our lives went on: work, night school and some play. At home we still had plenty of food, not realising that many did not. Some things got tighter, though in our village not very much changed.

For VJ Day we got two days off and celebrated as we had for VE Day – bonfires, food coming out of long hidden storage, feasting, drinking, kissing the girls, we danced in the streets as the dance halls were too packed to even try to get in, there were all-night parties; we found ourselves in unknown houses – who did they belong to? – but were made welcome, even more so when they found out I could play the family piano, broken keys and all. Many versions of 'Lili Marlene' (a German love song popular throughout World War II) sound much the same, with or without all the keys. The end? Not for most as austerity bit into the little that most people had.

We all thought the end of the war in Europe would bring things back to normality, but how wrong could we be?

Food got reduced as rations were cut. Bread had not been rationed in wartime but it was in July 1946, though my mother got the National flour and made her own bread. She said she could sift the muck out of it, as we never knew what went into the National Loaf; it was neither white nor brown but a sort of greyish colour along with wartime margarine: you had to be hungry to eat it. [The National Loaf had been introduced by the government as part of the home front in 1942. It was made with wholemeal flour with added calcium and vitamins. Mushy and unappetising, few preferred it to white bread. Bread rationing continued until July 1948, though the National Loaf was not abolished until 1956, even after food rationing in Britain officially ended in July 1954.]

People in big towns and cities had it much harder than we did in the villages with room for growing our own and having animals – most homes had a pig and hens' eggs could be stored in large stoneware tubs coated in isinglass, a type of gelatin.

You could open the tub to retrieve an egg months old, as fresh as the day it was put down. We got a box of goodies from our relatives in New Zealand every six months or so plus the half a frozen sheep we also received which arrived from the docks still frozen and had to be sawn up, then spread round the family, as we did not have fridges. It was thawed out and cooked long and slow for a delicious addition to our rations.

Us four apprentices would eat in the National Canteen in Alma Street, the St John's Hall where they fed workers from all around who did not have work canteens.

We got a main meal, pudding and pint of tea for fourpence as lads, and the grown-ups paid eight-pence, the price of a pint of beer.

It was good, wholesome food served by young girls who filled the plates of us lads to overflowing, all in return for a dance at the Palais on Saturday night. I never knew a vegetarian. We'd have thought a vegan some sort of Greek god: you ate when the food appeared and very little went to waste.

Clothes were still rationed and harder to get, though having a dressmaker mother meant we were always well clothed. She could get an old suit, take it apart, wash it, refresh the nap, then cut it and sew it into a new suit. [The nap describes the texture of the fabric, revealing which way the fibres align.] I even had a Raglan-style overcoat, very Beau Brummell. We went dancing in a suit, tie and dance shoes while the girls were in dresses or skirt and blouse.

Spivs abounded; it was a dirty word yet we all practised it. (Spiv is a slang word describing a petty criminal dealing in illicit, usually black-market goods.) The Canadians at Goosepool handed out Sweet Caporal Cigarettes by the hundred. (Goosepool was the area where RAF Bomber Command were stationed near Darlington.)

Mother and Dad smoked. I did not, but we had loads which I sold at work, the money going to the household income. Mother also got tinned fruit cake sent from Canada for the lads – who got sick of fruit cake and gave it away, but I never got sick of it. Half of one of those cakes, suitably decorated, would stand in for a wedding cake for the young couples getting married. It was all give and take, and we were all spivs in our own way.

Even the local bobby came to us for his few slices of bacon and a couple of our eggs.'

Frank Mee

## THE POST-WAR RATION CUTS

On 27 May, just three weeks after VE Day, cuts were made to the basic ration. Bacon rations were cut from 4 oz to 3 oz. Cooking fat rations were cut from 2 oz to 1 oz. Meat ration, meagre as it had been, was now to be taken in corned beef.

As Frank Mee outlined earlier, there was a vast contrast between the lives of families in more rural areas and those in the city. Food, shelter and education were totally different for the many city-dwelling families living in slum-type conditions. They'd managed, somehow, to come through the war, but very little was due to improve for them until the end of the 1940s – and beyond.

## 'WE'D BEEN LIVING OFF MR NOTHING'

Christopher Lambrianou was born in 1938, the eldest of three brothers. The family lived in the centre of London sharing part of a rented house in Howland Street, just off Tottenham Court Road. Today, the area surrounding the street is known as Fitzrovia, an upmarket enclave of offices and posh eating places. By the end of the war, it was still a very crowded, bombed-out inner-city area with slum type housing.

We lived at number 45 Howland Street. An early memory is going to a shop round the corner where they sold fruit and veg – where there were never ever any bananas.

As kids, you lived day to day, running into the underground station at Goodge Street to sleep on the platform – or sleep on the rails – in an air raid. There was a massive stuffed bear situated on the entrance of a furniture store facing Goodge Street station. You'd be running towards the tube and facing you was this big stuffed bear.

All around us in Howland Street – which is today close by the Post Office Tower – were tiny narrow streets, virtually alleyways. There was a blacksmith with a horse and cart in one of them. The horse was called Gallop Her Lightly and he would let me sit on the horse and ride with him in the cart as he went round shouting, 'Any Old Iron' – there was plenty of that after the bombings.

For us kids, the street party celebrations for VE and VJ day were amazing. Until then, we had been living off Mr Nothing. We ate a lot of bread and dripping, which was tasty, particularly the brown meaty stuff underneath the white stuff. To us, those street parties meant no more bombs, terror, or running away every night when the siren sent us off to the underground.

Everything came out on that table: all spread out were things like bread and marmalade, fresh fruit, cake, biscuits, nothing you ever normally saw – all black-market stuff – there were glasses of thick orange juice and real milk – all we were getting up till then was powdered milk.

You got the news from the radio, but we didn't have a proper radio set connected to the electricity, we had something that only worked off a battery, where you went to the shop taking the battery in, they would fill it and recharge it for a few pence, so then it would last for a couple of months. To us, even having a proper radio was a big deal. Sometimes if someone on the street had a radio in their house, they would shout out the news to let everyone know what was happening. Of course we hated the Germans; they were in the wrong, they started it. Italians too were badly thought of; they'd joined up with Hitler and Mussolini in the war.

Yet it was hard to understand it all as a kid. We had Italian kids at my school; they were Catholics. I couldn't understand why the adults kept saying they didn't like the Italians, because I thought they were kind people, so you understood at an early age that despite what the adults kept saying, not everyone was bad. But of course the news we heard more or less told us what to think: all that stuff about 'we will fight them on the beaches'. It existed to make us feel strong, even powerful. Even though some of us would be bombed to bits.

The thing was, I was not made to feel English, because I had a Greek name. When I was a bit older, I vividly remember going to someone's house and a woman saying, 'Don't bring the Greek kid again.'

To many people then foreigners were not wanted and treated with suspicion, both in the war and afterwards.

My dad was arrested at one point in the war. He'd missed the last bus back and was walking home when a warden jumped out, shouting, 'Where are you going?' He told them he'd just missed the bus but when they heard his accent, they immediately thought, 'He's a German spy,' and marched him to the police station. Luckily, the inspector knew my dad and said: 'German spy? It's Mr Lambrianou'. Another time, just after the war, my dad wound up arrested after killing a rat, pouring hot water over it in a restaurant to kill it. This was quickly reported to the authorities. He was a foreigner, so that was enough.

Foreigners didn't have an easy time after the war, Greeks, Italians, Jewish people, black people, they all came in for what we now call discrimination. Yet these people had left their country, and brought a good culture with them. My dad left Cyprus in the 1930s and came to

London like so many to make a life, and work. They didn't come to England for benefits – in any event there were no benefits then. They just came to work and they worked hard. England greeted them and the people employing them were often foreigners themselves, people who had come to England and done well. So they employed the newer people.

At age seven, just as it was ending, we'd got right through the bombing – the West End of London was massacred – with bomb sites all around us. People had run away leaving everything in the house, so as kids we would sometimes go and play in these bombed-out places, no thought that the roof might cave in: the bomb damage was horrendous, it smashed everything. We were lucky the house we were living in didn't get a hit but most of the others around us did.

But one day I came home from school and the roof of our house caved in, so they moved us all into a work-house in south London, though my dad had to find other accommodation, a rule of the workhouse.

We stayed in the workhouse for two to three months. We came out after the war had ended then they moved us from the workhouse to a place where my brother Lee and I slept in a dormitory with fifty men.

We were in there for about four months, then we went to a halfway house in Victoria, a posh house converted for families. There we had one big room between all of us. We were there for six months. Then we were sent to

Hackney and the local authority gave us a flat: Belford House, Queensbridge Road.

To us it was amazing, a place with hot running water. So we stayed there for much of our lives, and my dad, Chris, stayed there until he died aged eighty-three: Belford House is still there, still standing.

Schooling changed a lot for kids like us. I loved going to St James's School, Spanish Place, then I wound up in St Patrick's, Soho – still there – that was where I was moved to when the roof caved in. But by us moving again I wound up in another school in Victoria, then yet another school in Hackney.

For years afterwards, I'd think about that school in Spanish Place and how much I loved it. You do wonder: would life have turned out differently if I'd got the education I could have had if the war hadn't turned everything upside down?

As I researched this book, Christopher Lambrianou's recall of the racist attitudes at that time towards anyone that wasn't English reminded me of my father, Ginger. He came from an East End Cockney background: his family had lived in 'The Lane' (Petticoat Lane in Spitalfields) for over a hundred years.

In trawling through some old wartime black-and-white photos kept by my mother, I found a stunning example of this casual racism. Ginger spent the last year of the war in the Pay Corps in Meerut, India. Scrawled on the back of one photo of Ginger and two others at a racetrack he had written: 'One of the lads and my wog assistant' as a description.

Cockney slang or argot was part of my dad's verbosity. But nonetheless, it was revealing to see how verbally unrestrained the wartime soldier would be when it came to describing the millions who lived in the Dominions.

It wasn't just Cockney Londoners who felt that way. Even in London's quieter middle-class suburbs, wartime attitudes, including those of scrimping and saving, lingered on for many years.

### 'MUM WOULD HAND OUT SHOP-SOILED GREEN £1 NOTES EVEN AFTER THEY WERE NO LONGER LEGAL TENDER.'

Michael Proom grew up in Orpington, Kent, in a semi-detached house with a long, wide back garden. He was just two years old when World War II ended.

My earliest memory is lying in my pram on the verandah of our house and seeing the sky turn dark with indistinct shapes. Later I learned that these had been Bomber aircraft assembling at the nearby RAF base at Biggin Hill to meet with their fighter aircraft before leaving to bomb Germany.

Dig for Victory' was the creed during the war. [The huge Dig for Victory educational campaign was set up by the Ministry of Agriculture to encourage everyone to grow their own food in times of rationing.]

At home we always had fresh apples for part of the year; we wrapped the remainder in newspaper and kept them in the dark depths of the coal cellar for the winter. We grew our own fresh vegetables and tomatoes and even had grapes to eat in the summer. Down the back garden was the air-raid shelter – not just any old Nissen hut for us, but a good, solid concrete shelter, the walls sunk into the earth and three steps down, turn right to the blast-proof area. I can still smell the dank mustiness of that shelter.

Orpington had remained essentially immune from the ravages of more than five years of war. We lived a peaceful, quiet existence. It was a solid, respectable and especially a safe middle-class enclave. This semi-pastoral peace and quiet was severely shaken on the morning of 27 March 1945, when the last German rocket to hit Britain fell on Kynaston Road, less than a mile from our home.

Had it not been for the rear wall of the Carlton cinema nearby taking the brunt of the blast, there would have been many deaths if it had struck when the cinema was full of filmgoers, Amazingly, only one person, an unlucky housewife, was killed.

From 1941 until 1954, food, clothing, petrol and furniture were all strictly rationed. Rationing became even more severe after war ended.

In 1947–8 there was a national paper shortage. Schools would ask children to use very small writing. Ink was of the poorest quality so the end result was often impossible to read. Like millions of wives, Mum had to become a seamstress and take up knitting to clothe the family from old clothes. In the shops, utility clothing that used a minimum of cloth was also introduced. No scrap of material was ever thrown away. I was eleven when rationing finally ended, but by then there had been shortages for almost fourteen years. That left a profound and indelible impression on most wives and mothers which would stay with them for the rest of their days. It certainly affected my mother for the rest of her life.

What we would today consider meanness was for her probably simply precautionary – in case the Hun, as they called the Germans, ever came back. Over subsequent years she had always given me, my brother Phil and her grandkids what can only be described as jumble-sale knick-knacks for our birthdays and Christmases. Either a plastic toy car with a 6d. price tag on the bottom for my son or for Phil a tartan 'tam-o'-shanter' that looked like it had belonged to Harry Lauder, the internationally renowned Scottish singer.

Second-hand clothes two sizes too big went to my wife and daughter. My mother also seemed to have an endless supply of shop-soiled green £1 notes – which she continued to hand out to family members long after they had ceased to become legal tender in 1988.

Talking with friends today they all report the same traits in their own mothers: over-careful with money, throwing nothing away, reusing materials and so forth. The result of scrimping and hoarding and making ends meet in the war, while always wondering when the bomb with their family's name on it might arrive. Fourteen years of that left an indelible scar on the psyche.

Michael Proon's own wartime experience was nothing like that of my dad or Christopher Lambrianou, yet he vividly recalled the post-war cultural attitudes towards anyone 'foreign'.

He remembered, 'We had all been brought up to believe that we Brits were somehow superior, not just to those in the colonies, but to Turks, Italians – even the Froggies as we called them.

'Superiority and xenophobia ruled in our island stronghold. We had a tacit social apartheid that was understood by all of us. We just took it for granted that we were somehow superior to everyone else. We had won the war, hadn't we?

## CHAPTER 3

# LIVING THROUGH THE WAR

*'The only thing we have to fear is fear itself'*
FRANKLIN D ROOSEVELT.

The oft-repeated 'spirit of the Blitz' is an honest perspective of Britain in World War II. Yet other, less widely reported factors, are often overlooked in Britain's wartime history.

One example is that in wartime, crime statistics rose. The crime rate on the home front rose by 57 per cent through war years, a combination of illegal black marketing, looting of bombed premises, forged ration cards, robbery – and even in extreme cases, murder.

One of the 1950s' most notorious crime bosses, Billy Hill (1911–84), confirmed how he relished the black market in his autobiography, *Boss of Britain's Underworld*.

Hill had been released from prison around the time war broke out in 1939. A professional crook, he profited enormously from wartime criminal activity. Gangs organised by Hill pulled off a series of audacious wartime smash-and-grab robberies on some of London's most expensive jewellery stores.

In his autobiography Hill wrote: 'I did not pose as a patriotic citizen. Britain's wartime black market was the most fantastic side of civilian life in wartime.'

'I did not merely make use of the black market. I fed it.'

Opportunity for crime thrived during war. The blackout, with every household ordered to cover all light from the home to make it more difficult for the bombers to target, meant there was no street lighting at all.

Pitch-dark streets created chaos, especially following bombing raids. Police forces were depleted, many forces losing good, experienced officers to the military.

Thieves were known to sport ARP helmets and armbands as a disguise – in order to help themselves from bomb-damaged shops and homes. (Some 1.4 million ARP wardens, mostly part-time volunteers with full-time jobs elsewhere, patrolled the streets during the blackout. Their role was also to report the extent of bomb damage and support those using public air-raid shelters.)

The government established a fund to pay compensation to those who had completely lost their homes. It could be as much as £500 (worth over £20,000 today). This too was a temptation too far for the criminally minded. One man, Walter Handy, claimed he had been 'bombed out' nineteen times during the war and profited the proceeds. He received three years' jail for his efforts to cash in.

The bombing raids and the blackout also provided perfect cover for murder. Gordon Cummins, the 'Blackout Ripper', was a twenty-eight-year-old RAF aircraftman, known by friends in the RAF as 'The Count' because of his lofty pretentions to a noble background.

In February 1942, in a period of six days, Cummins stalked London's blacked-out streets and murdered four women. Evelyn Hamilton, forty, was found strangled to death in an air-raid shelter in London's West End. Evelyn Oatley, thirty-five, was found naked in her Soho flat the following day. She had been strangled, her throat cut and she had been sexually mutilated. The day after that, Mrs Margaret Lowe, forty-three, was also found strangled in her flat in London's West End, her body also mutilated. The pathologist described the murderer as 'a savage sexual maniac'. One day later, Mrs Doris Jouannet was found strangled in the London flat she shared with her husband, a hotel manager. She too had been mutilated.

The next day an attack in London's Piccadilly – on a woman whose attacker had been interrupted by a delivery boy making his rounds – led to a lucky escape and an important clue.

The attacker, running off, had dropped a service gas mask bearing a number on the side of its container. Even before police could trace the owner of the number, another woman was attacked near Paddington railway station, but she also escaped safely.

Two days later, on 16 February, police traced the number on the container – and arrested Gordon Cummins. Searching his home, they found various incriminating items belonging to his victims. Cummins was found guilty of the murders and executed in June 1942 at Wandsworth Prison – during an air raid.

Other cases were also notable during these dark nights. During the Blitz in April 1941, Londoner Harry Dobkin strangled his estranged wife, Rachel, and dumped her body under the ruin of Vauxhall Baptist Chapel, hoping she would be seen as a victim of an air raid. (Dobkin had already noted that following an air raid, victims tended to be buried quickly and very few post-mortems were carried out.)

Rachel's body was not discovered until May 1942. A pathologist was called in and the examination revealed that the victim had been strangled, her head decapitated. In August that year, Dobkin was arrested. Following a trial in November, Dobkin confessed to Rachel's murder claiming that she was always pestering him for money and he wanted to be rid of her for good. He was executed in London's Wandsworth Prison in January 1943.

But aside from those headline-grabbing cases, food rationing fraud, i.e. black marketing, as already mentioned, was the main criminal issue.

The government had set out different types of ration books for different sections of the population. The rationale around rationing was to feed everyone, rich and poor alike, based on scientific principles on nutrition. Yet feeding 48 million people in a fair manner was complex.

Amounts per person had to be strictly controlled, and customers had to register with a shop to buy food – yet the shops often didn't have enough food to go round. For example, the Ministry of Food offered alternatives to rationed foods like bacon, which had been one of the first items to be rationed. One alternative offer was described as 'macon' (mutton dressed as bacon, tasting quite awful).

Yet it was the rationing of other everyday items that provoked the most dismay as war went on.

Tomatoes, for instance, became hard to come by, so popular household brands like Heinz Tomato Ketchup vanished. By 1942, severe food shortages had become a way of life as increasing numbers of foods had to be rationed (including sweets).

As a consequence, the black marketeers proliferated in the cities and increasing numbers of people were tempted to take advantage of the black market, knowing full well it was illegal.

Looting also went on in large measure. Nearly 5,000 looting cases went before the judiciary in London's Old Bailey, the main criminal court, at the end of 1940.

Occupants of bombed-out homes would return to discover that the smouldering ruins had been stripped of any surviving valuables.

Looters were not always criminals or even ordinary people – air-raid wardens, firemen and other members of the home defence forces were tempted to rob their fellow men or women.

When wartime's most glamorous London nightclub and restaurant, the Café de Paris, took a direct hit in March 1941, the bomb killed thirty-four people and injured eighty others.

The upmarket Café in London's Coventry Street had been allowed to stay open in order to inject some glamour into the Blitz. Its clientele was made up of a combination of the wealthy and beautiful, off-duty servicemen and women and ordinary young people. For three hours rescuers combed the debris by moonlight, often having to chase off opportunist looters fighting each other in order to strip the dead bodies of their jewellery.

## 'THE MORE DARING OF US WOULD SCOUR THE RUINS LOOKING FOR A CORPSE'

Inner-city children in bombed-out areas were caught up in this type of crime. Ron Piper was a seven-year-old when he began low-level looting of bomb sites in London. Born in 1935, Ron lived with his family in the area around Marylebone. His father was in the armed forces. For Ron and his friends, the bombings of the war meant tremendous excitement more than anything else.

So there was a war going on, but to me as a seven-year-old boy, it didn't matter.

People dying, being wounded, bombs falling all over London, blasting homes to the ground, it was no great fuss. What it had done for me was to fetch an excitement to my life, the bombed houses becoming dangerous playgrounds to be searched for anything that could be taken home as legitimate booty. All sorts of things were found by the gang of kids I hung around with (mainly boys, with a few girls now and again).

There was money and the odd bit of jewellery which we gave to our mothers (the jewellery that is, the odd bit of money we kept quiet about) but the most important find of all was shrapnel. Shrapnel was something that could be bartered with: the bigger the piece, the more that was offered by other kids who had not been so lucky in their search. A whole week's sweet ration could be asked for and got. So the hunt was on each day.

During these hunts things could become a bit macabre, especially after a night-time air raid, a night spent by whole families in the crypt of the local church, used as an air-raid shelter. Emerging from the church to go back home after the all-clear had sounded, eyes were everywhere, looking for fires still burning, seeking out houses that had taken direct hits. As the day progressed, we kids knew we would be searching these bomb-damaged buildings for whatever could be found, to take home as our booty for the day.

In our search for goods amongst the ruins, at times talk went on between us that there could be a dead body under the rubble. So the more daring of us would scour the ruins looking for a corpse.

There was an awful dread inside me that one day we would uncover one. Goodness knows what would have happened if we did. I'm sure that the dead body would have been surrounded by the bodies of a gang of children who had died of fright.

With my best mate Dave, searching a bombed house we found a tailor's dummy, which we buried beneath some rubble. We then let it be known, amongst the gang of kids we got around with, that we thought we knew where there was a body. Followed by the gang we took them to our burial ground. Once there we gave them all a different spot to search, keeping our secret spot for ourselves. Pretending to dig we kept a careful eye on the others, who very reluctantly were searching amongst the rubble.

'Over here!' Dave and I pointed to the ground at our feet. A deadly hush went over the ruins. The others seemed to have a sickly look about them to me. A few shouted back 'What is it?'

'A dead body,' we replied. They all took a couple of steps back and called, 'Let's call the police,' but Dave and I were having none of that, and called back,

'You're all yeller!'

Gradually we coaxed them over and pointed to the dummy's hand sticking up from the ground. Little screams and gasps of shock went up around us. Bending down I grasped the hand and with a tug pulled it from the ground and then threw it in the direction of the kids. Shouting and screaming they fled from the bomb site, leaving Dave and myself laughing, fit to bust. That is until later, when the parents of these other kids came round to our houses to complain about what we had done. They had even reported us to the police, who came round to ask us where the body was. So Dave and I had to explain what we had done. Although we got a severe warning from the local bobby, I swear I saw the glimmer of a smile on his face. After that we gave up our search for the dead, real or otherwise.

The crypt of the church I mentioned earlier was below the church that had the same name as the school we should have been attending each day, Christ Church.

But no kids since then have had a better excuse not to go to school than we did.

Our sleep disturbed by air raids during the night, we needed our sleep the following day. That is until our mums had gone to work, quite happy that we were fast asleep and safe from harm. As soon as they were out of the door then so were we, out to the bomb sites to see what we could discover.

London in 1942 was full of troops from all the services but most appeared to be American. Much later in the 1970s a sitcom was made called *Yanks Go Home*; at the time I thought they were home.

They seemed to be everywhere, on the streets, in the

pubs and parks, in the homes of some of my friends and even in my own home.

My mother worked as a vegetable cook in one of the American service's NAAFIs, which was situated at the back of Marble Arch. [A NAAFI was a company created by the British government to run recreational establishments needed by the British Armed Forces and to sell goods to servicemen and their families.]

Once a week my brother, sister and I had to walk from where we lived, about a mile and a half away, to this NAAFI and tell the soldier on guard at the door that we had come to see our mum. Once he and the other soldiers got used to us calling each week they let us in automatically and out again.

My mother knew exactly what she was doing on the days we had to meet her at work. It coincided with the day the soldiers drew their weekly rations. This was always in the mornings, so us three kids had to time our entry for lunchtime. Then we would sit, surrounded by soldiers eating, who themselves were surrounded by packages of cigarettes, sweets and toiletries. All things that, because of the war, were in short supply – but not to these American servicemen it would seem. After a while, soldiers would come over to us and give us packets of sweets. They even gave us toiletries. Perhaps they thought we needed them as usually we had come straight from the bomb sites where we had been playing and so were a scruffy looking trio.

After all the servicemen had left the dining hall having finished their meals, my mother would come over to us and take away all the things we had been given.

She would then disappear and after a short while would come back with everything in a carrier bag. She would then give us strict orders to go straight home with it, which we always did. On getting home we would unpack the carrier, share out the sweets and then put away the tin of corned beef, cheese, tea and whatever my mother had hidden away under our sweets. After all, who would search three scruffy kids leaving a military building, carrying sweets given to them by soldiers?

My father was away serving in the Army and we saw little of him for quite a while. So discipline was at a premium, which suited us kids. My father, if anyone, was the person who had any control over my brother, sister and me. One word from him and we did exactly what we were told. With him there was no such thing as the heavy hand being at all appropriate to use on us kids, he never had the need. He had such an air about him that he made his word law in our household. This applied not only to us kids but also to our mother.

With my mother though, it was a completely different story. She would whack us at the drop of a hat and not hold back with the weight of her fist or feet. Unfortunately for her and us it didn't work. We stood up to the beltings she gave us, where we could not do this to the look of our father.

Where we lived would today be considered a slum area, but there was no one who seemed to care enough to do anything about it. We three kids shared a three-room flat in a house in a back street of Marylebone; a house that was shared with six other families. Our flat had one very tiny room that was my sister's bedroom, and the one that my brother and I shared also did duty as the kitchen and sitting room.

Trying to sleep was a virtual impossibility. My mother liked to hold court with her friends over endless cups of tea. There they would sit and gossip for hours on end, at times into the early hours of the morning.

Before my father went into the Army he wouldn't stand for much of this and somewhat tersely would tell her friends it was time for them to go, a thing he and my mother had continual rows over.

But now he was away she had her own way and she and her friends would natter away until the small hours. I would lie there listening until sheer tiredness sent me to sleep. One of my favourite things to do, as I lay there listening, was to pick at the wallpaper as I knew that I would uncover a bug. The whole house was running alive with them. They all seemed to live just beneath the surface of the wallpaper. So there I would lie, picking away until I uncovered one.

Then I would remove it to just where I wanted it to be and then crush it under my thumb nail. Each night I would not be satisfied until I had squashed at least half a dozen of these bugs. I had to be very careful in my hunt for them because if my mother caught me I was sure to get a wallop around the head, as she always imagined that if no one disturbed the bugs they would stay behind the wallpaper out of sight.

Of course we kids had different gangs. The one I was in was made up mainly from the street we lived in. We had a Tarzan-like yodel or yell to call gang members together, either from home or other streets. Perhaps Tarzan got to know of our call and stole our copyright.

Each gang had its own den, club, meeting place or whatever. Ours was in the basement of a house that had had a direct hit from a bomb. We had it laid out with old furniture from other ruins. Old chairs and tables, even a battered settee with the guts spewing out of it, and lit by candles we had nicked from home. And of course we put an old blanket up over the window as it was a time of blackout and we didn't want the ARP warden coming round spotting the light and kicking our arses out of our headquarters.

Ration book fraud was also a profitable enterprise for fraudsters and thieves. In 1944 a gang in the north of England stole 14,000 newly issued ration books, selling them on the black market for a profit of £70,000 (£3m today).

Forged clothing coupons (clothing was first rationed in June 1941 using a points system with coupons) could be sold on the black market for £10 each (£400 today). These were widely circulated in London.

Aside from petty thievery and fraud, war-related crime came in other unexpected forms, too. For instance, there were those who were strongly opposed to war and, whilst opinions vary as to whether their refusal to sign up for military service equates with criminality (it was, after all, a moral choice as much as anything else), it was a prosecutable offence.

During World War I (1914–18) around 16,000 men refused to join military service. Six thousand of these COs (conscientious objectors) were arrested and imprisoned for their refusal to join the battle.

In July 1916, a scheme set up by the Home Office allowed COs to leave prison in order to work in labour camps around the country. Some refused this, believing it continued to help the war effort they were so strongly opposed to.

COs were highly criticised during World War I, and afterwards the military claimed that such men were cowards. But their beliefs were far more complex than that, and after World War I a strong pacifist movement had developed in the UK through the 1920s and 1930s.

In World War II there were an estimated 60,000 COs (or 'Conchis' as they were known). Many of these were officially exempt as COs because they worked in 'protected' or reserved occupation areas, i.e. farmers, agricultural workers, teachers, doctors, engineers, or in Civil Defence areas like the Home Guard or the ARP.

Attitudes to refusal to fight had shifted: less than 4,000 COs were sent to prison. Public opinion against them was kinder than it had been in the previous war. Yet there were pockets of resentment, especially in small rural areas.

## 'YOUR DAD'S A CONCHI!'

Judy Williams was born in 1938 in Hook Norton, a small village in Oxfordshire. Her father, Tom, was a farmer, with a small eighty-acre farm with cows and vegetables.

Judy was the second eldest of four, with two sisters and one brother.

I remember the planes flying towards Coventry. Our village was on the flight path. Every night you could hear the low drone of the planes going over.

Our father Tom was part of a large group in the area called the Popular Front. [The Popular Front was a 1930s coalition of different political groups, formed to challenge the pre-war government led by Neville Chamberlain.]

A farmer's son, he'd won a grammar school place and had ideas for university but he quickly decided he preferred rural life.

I was very aware that my dad was a pacifist, what they called a 'conscientious objector'. I was quite proud of it. The people in our village had mixed feelings about his pacifism. He was very involved in village life and they disliked him for that.

One of my earliest childhood memories is running away from school with kids shouting at me, 'Your dad's a conchie!' But as kids in the family, we were of the same mind as our dad. Though it was hard for our mother, she was the local midwife. So it was a very peculiar situation.

Later in life, I realised that some people felt bad about my dad not being in the military because it was their sons who were away fighting, being killed. So dad was one of the people they could take their fury out on. As a child, of course, you wouldn't realise that. But a lot of their fury was about their own and other people's loss.

We'd hear about the war on the radio and when I was three we had an influx of evacuees coming to live alongside us; half a dozen children and their parents lived in a cottage on our farmland. They lived there for the whole of the war – and after. Living on a farm we had plenty of food; we had rabbits, hens – and ration books.

My mum had an older sister in London whom we called Auntie Phil; she lived in Brixton, south London, with her husband and two children. During the war she had come to see us – but we didn't go there, of course.

My memory of the end of the war in 1945 was a Victory march through our village. All the kids had little Union Jack flags. I wasn't allowed to participate but I was naughty enough to pinch a few pennies from my gran's money and bought a flag to wave anyway. I just wanted to do what all the other kids were doing, the only time I ever pinched any money.

It must have been around 1947 when my sister Pat, my mum and I went to visit Auntie Phil, a train ride to

Paddington station then a tube trip to the Oval, followed by a bus ride to Brixton. The war was over so we were looking forward to seeing her – and London.

What a shock we got on arrival. We walked along the road to her house and it was just ... a pile of bricks! No houses, just bricks and rubble. I was amazed; and horrified. We had no idea what had happened to create these great big mountains of bricks, though fortunately auntie's house was still standing.

I felt very frightened at the idea that all these houses had been demolished. I don't think I understood the implication of war and what it really meant until that day. All I can remember is the horror of it. All we'd known was fields and animals. Innocence.

Yes, we had evacuees from London living with us but I didn't put together the connection with the evacuees living with us – Hook Norton itself had about 200 – to what I saw that day, that this was the truth of where they'd come from.

In our family, we had a sense that it was right not to go to war. Yet seeing what it could do with my own eyes brought home the reality of it all.

Judy's story and the various accounts of criminality were, in one respect, the 'hidden' or darker aspects of wartime. Yet there were also inspiring and life-affirming wartime positives. For example, rationing meant food shortages all the time – yet the rationing had been planned so that there were also healthy and nutritious non-rationed foods available. Fish, fresh vegetables, offal, flour and oatmeal were never rationed.

Furthermore, school meals were extended during the war, encouraging women to go into wartime jobs. In 1940, there were 130,000 school meals in Britain. By 1945, 1,650,000 school meals were provided.

And relating to schools, the Education Act of 1944, introduced that year, was also a hugely significant signpost for the post-war world.

Education, especially in the larger cities, received many severe blows during wartime thanks to evacuation, commandeering of school buildings, destruction of schools from bombing and call-up for teachers into the Forces.

Addressing the country's educational needs via demands for social reform had, in fact, been an issue even before World War II began. As the war went on, some children did receive a good education – but many more lost out.

## 'NEVER DID WE THINK WE WOULDN'T WIN'

Lillian Hills was born in 1928 and grew up in the Woolwich area, south London, with her parents and a brother.

When war broke out the children were both evacuated to schools away from London. Lillian was evacuated with her school (Roan School for Girls, a charitably funded grammar school) to Bexhill-on-Sea, Sussex.

Her education was typical of secondary school wartime pupils where the ongoing threat of invasion meant frequently moving pupils and school to different parts of the country. Fortunately, in Lillian's case, she had a classical education and was able to continue her studies to the age of sixteen.

My first billet in Bexhill was with three other girls in a large house with a maid.

We were only there for a week then moved to Cooden, the posh end of Bexhill, in another large house owned by two Scottish ladies. We shared the grammar school for half the day, the rest being spent in the museum, various halls or in the music room.

The long promenade had us all buying skates and we would go to the beach with our teachers and swim. The school was up on the Downs.

Christmas came and although missing our families we were given a good time by our hostesses. Sadly, the ladies sold up and went back to Scotland, and I was then billeted with a family with a girl about my age.

That winter was very cold and water being short we would have a stone hot water bottle then used the water from it to wash in the next morning!

Lots of snow had us on trays sledging. We would skate on the frozen pond in the park too.

Then life became much more serious with the fall of France. I remember reading the news on the school noticeboard. Strangely, we felt we knew where we were then – Britain on its own – but never did we think we wouldn't win.

Soon we were moved to Ammanford in South Wales and a very different life.

Sundays especially were very strictly observed. I was billeted with the local chapel minister and his wife – she was nice but he was very sarcastic.

We were lucky to have a school abandoned but serviceable on our own, with visits to the local grammar school for science lessons. There was also a chapel for music, affectionately known as Zion Zinc because of the tin roof. There was a large playing field nearby for hockey and cricket, although the local railway line provided a distraction at times.

Our classical education was not neglected with visits from Dame Sybil Thorndike and Lewis Casson in *Medea*, Benjamin Britten with *Peter Grimes* and another troupe playing *Twelfth Night*. We would also be taken to the Gower coast. Langland Bay was most beautiful.

There was a broadcast on Welsh radio called 'We Come Along You' about evacuees. Some of our girls spoke and the rest of us sang. Ammanford also had a cinema changing films twice a week and a welfare hall showing films too.

I was a frequent visitor.

Donald Peers was a popular Welsh singer at the time. He had a son there who ran the local youth club which was popular.

I was then moved on nearer the centre of town, again the home of another minister. Although the house was larger I was sharing a single bed with another girl. Each morning we had to bring down everything we wanted for the day and were not allowed to go back upstairs for anything. We were served stinging nettle soup but refused it. [A widely known flowering plant, rich in vitamin C and iron, nettles have a long history as a source of traditional medicine. Tea made with steeping nettle leaves has been regarded as a tonic.]

Getting older I went home for a visit during the Blitz, which set most of Docklands on fire. I was very frightened and wondered how my mother could stand it, what with my father working in the police at the Woolwich Arsenal (one of the country's largest munitions factories) and my brother and me being so far away.

Back to school and we were doing our School Certificate exams. Despite all our changes and upheavals we passed! We ended the school year with a sports day with all the local schools – Roan won and marked a fitting end to my schooldays and time in Wales.

Later I joined the Royal Arsenal Research Department, sometimes seeing my father in the RA police on Plumstead Gate. Work was very hectic with new designs being tested and proved on the big guns – no complaints about noise in those days!

Thankfully peace was finally declared. Our relief was great but tinged with sadness at the loss of so many lives.

Other wartime positives included:

- CHILDREN. Infant mortality fell substantially during the war.
- FAMILY. The Family Allowance Bill, the first-ever law to provide child benefit in the UK, was enacted in June 1945 (under the then Conservative government). The Allowance provided families with five shillings a week for each child; it came into operation in August 1946.
- HEALTH AWARENESS Lively government propaganda through the war served to improve health awareness: poster campaigns like 'Coughs and Sneezes Spread Diseases' meant that many people became far more aware of the basic rules of health.
- CANTEENS were developed in schools and in large factories, also 'British Restaurants' (as mentioned by Frank Mee) which sprang up in smaller factory and office areas, all serving nutritious food midday at cheap prices, a welcome addition to ration book fare.

## 'I LINED UP FOR OVER TWO HOURS FOR TOMATOES AND STILL DIDN'T GET ANY'

In 1941, teenage Joyce Bishop from Dartford, Kent, was working at the Crayford Civil Defence Department at the town hall. She explains:

Foods like offal, rabbit, fish and suchlike were unrationed. Canned food was on points, i.e. a tin of sausage meat cost sixteen points, a tin of fruit salad eight points. Dried egg was a fair substitute for real eggs. I queued up for one-and-a-quarter hours for the first oranges and toma- toes – queueing up became the norm – and once I lined up for over two hours for tomatoes and still didn't get any.

The British Restaurant in Waterside, Kent, was very popular. Mrs Grundy was the supervisor and a two-course meal was available for one shilling. It augmented the meat and fat ration. A typical meal would be roast beef, vegetables and apple tart. There was little choice, but one day you might get boiled bacon, chips and peas or perhaps liver, chips and beans. We some- times had to queue twenty minutes to get in, and on at least one occasion my diary noted that I still felt hungry after my meal.

Communication, of course, was crucial. How did people receive news of the war? Popular newspapers like the *Daily Express*, *Daily Mirror*, *Daily Mail*, *Sunday Express*, *News of the World* had established readers in the millions, though a shortage of newsprint in 1940 meant lower circulations and thinner paper quality. (The newsprint shortage also meant that books too were printed in closer type, making them harder to read – and with limited availability.)

Today we have a huge number of mass communication channels at our fingertips. During World War II television did not exist at all. Just 20,000 TV sets had been in exist- ence in homes when war broke out, yet all were shut down in

September 1939, only to recommence broadcasting in 1946 with just one BBC channel with tiny audiences: TV sets did not become widely available for ordinary people until 1953, the year of the TV broadcast of Queen Elizabeth II's coronation.

Essentially, there were two key communication channels that shaped people's perceptions of the war at every stage. The first were cinemas and newsreels. The war years are often described as a golden era for the cinema in Britain. Popular entertainment in the cinema was, at times, thinly disguised wartime propaganda in the form of cinematic drama, yet with cinema audiences of 30 million a week by the end of 1945, the wartime 'message' gave audiences a combination of pleasure, escapism, a chance to forget the daily grind and, in some cases, served to reinforce the Allied determination to defeat Nazi Germany. Sometimes audiences could be more sharply affected by what they saw on the screen than by the conditions they were living through outside.

Eighty per cent of films watched by wartime audiences were American yet the war also saw a great revival in British cinema. The all-time cinema blockbuster of the war turned out to be *Gone with the Wind* which opened in 1939, an American Civil War epic with Clark Gable and Vivien Leigh, and the other Judy Garland classic, *The Wizard of Oz*, arrived that same year, just after war broke out. Other cinematic distractions included Charlie Chaplin's *The Great Dictator* (1940); Noel Coward's patriotic homage to the British

Navy, *In Which We Serve* (1942); and Laurence Olivier's *Henry V* (1944).

Newsreels were essentially filmed news events, Pathé News was shown in cinemas in between each programme, giving cinema audiences some (usually censored) cinematic news of war at home and overseas. There were also small newsreel cinemas in towns and cities. These had been in existence since the 1930s.

The second was radio from the BBC, the chief form of news and entertainment, at home and overseas. Listening to the radio increased hugely in wartime for an important combination of information and morale. Many families had already formed a radio 'habit' in the 1930s. By 1945 there were nearly 10 million radio licences in Britain (a precursor of BBC's TV licence). The BBC had complete broadcasting monopoly with two main programmes, the Home Service and the Forces Programme.

BBC shortwave broadcasts overseas had been deliberately planned to encourage audiences outside Britain. By the end of 1940, the BBC was broadcasting in thirty-four different languages; news bulletins in Denmark and Norway began on the days the two countries were invaded by Germany, and the Dutch service began a month after Holland was occupied. By the time of Germany's defeat in 1945, the BBC was broadcasting across the globe in forty-five languages.

As a tertiary channel of communication, the Home Service was launched on 1 September 1939 when war broke out.

Launched as a national service – a merger of two 1920s BBC Radio services, BBC National and BBC Regional – it aired from 7am each day until a quarter past midnight with half a dozen main news bulletins broadcast throughout the day.

The Forces Programme was launched in January 1940 and was originally intended for soldiers, though listeners at home received it. Earlier in the war, radio fans at home had tuned in to stations like Radio Hamburg to hear the German propaganda broadcasts of Lord Haw-Haw, William Joyce. (Joyce, who broadcast Nazi propaganda through the war was executed for treason in London in 1946, the last person to be executed for treason in the UK.)

The BBC introduction of the Forces Programme was partially in response to this. The Forces Programme quickly became more popular than the Home Service, because its output was less serious, mainly light entertainment with comedy, popular music, quiz shows and variety as well as news bulletins. Restrictions on the timing of news broadcasts were dropped at times of the country's need and the nine o'clock news became a fixed point in family life, everyone gathering round the Bakelite or wooden-encased set in the living room to listen.

*Forces Favourites*, a half-hour record request programme designed to link families at home with overseas Forces, started broadcasting in 1941. In 1945 it was succeeded by *Family Favourites* with a huge following through the 1950s and 1960s. It broadcast on the BBC network until 1984.

Two of the most popular wartime entertainment broadcasts were: *ITMA* (*It's That Man Again*) (1939–49), starring Tommy Handley. This comedy half hour became, in a way, the social glue of wartime Britain, its humour often related to wartime news. Launched on the Home Service in 1939, with its wacky characters like Mona Lott and Colonel Chinstrap, *ITMA* was a morale booster for the nation.

Also getting high ratings was *Music While You Work* on the daytime Forces radio. It broadcast continuous popular music twice a day on workdays.

A legendary broadcasting staple, it remained on air from June 1940 to September 1967, showcasing all kinds of popular music, light orchestras, dance bands with bandleaders like Jack Payne and Henry Hall, brass and military bands and, most significantly, the popular singers of the day.

Specifically set up to encourage workers in factories to be more productive, the programme became the backdrop to millions of factory workers, often singing along to the words of the popular songs of the time.

Frank Mee remembers it well.

It was broadcast through speakers in all the factories, big and small, after I started work from December 1944 onwards.

Eric Coates and his *Calling All Workers* was a must. (Coates (1886–1957) was the undisputed king of British light music, a composer and conductor who had created the *Music While You Work* signature tune.)

It was also played in canteens during lunch breaks in the larger factories I worked in later, like ICI, Nuffield, Dorman Long. We also had live music in the canteen at lunchtime.

I saw Dame Myra Hess play to a hushed crowd in Nuffield's canteen one lunchtime; you could have heard a pin drop. Quite a few times we had top-line performers there doing lunchtime concerts.

The *Music While You Work* programme was always upbeat singalong stuff.

We all sang along over the noise of crashing machinery, riveting and hammering. It was funny, you could walk across from one workshop to another and never miss a beat.

One band that stuck with me was The Banjoliers because I had a banjo as well as a piano and accordion. So I was a big hit at parties.

Dancing had been my love from watching Mother and Dad dancing for prizes at the local Co-op Hall from an early age, my own dancing classes with the Cochrane School of Dancing and the unforgettable Ruby who taught me Latin dancing: 'Come close, touch my bones, feel the rhythm of my body, now dance!' – heady stuff for a fifteen-year-old!

When I started work I was persuaded to go to the local Palais de Dance by the lads. I went into the dance hall at 7.30 to find none of the lads, just a lot of girls. I could dance, so got passed from one to another, barely sitting down.

Come the interval a couple of girls bought me a tea and bun then all the lads turned up from the pub.

I got a lecture. 'You go to the pub, have a few pints, then come to the dance with an eye on the girl you want to take home.'

*'Yeah, right,'* I thought. Then Florrie from the dance class, one of the older girls, walked over saying, 'Come on, Frank, let's show them how.' I left a lot of chins on the floor and questions as to how I did that, getting the third degree when I got back to the lads. Then even more so as a girl in uniform came up saying, 'You promised me a dance.'

It was talked about next day at work, I can tell you.

The dance music stayed in my memory as I was often asked to play it, favourites like 'In the Mood', 'Take the A Train', 'Chattanooga Choo Choo', 'Lili Marlene', 'I've Heard That Song Before' (Harry James and his Orchestra), 'Amapola' (a 1920s' Spanish song), 'Woodchopper's Ball', 'Rum and Coca Cola', 'You Are My Sunshine', 'You Made Me Love You', 'Pistol Packin' Mama', 'Blues in the Night', 'South of the Border', 'Boogie Woogie Bugle Boy', along with all the other wartime hits. 'The Lambeth Walk' as a group dance never lost its popularity even years later.

When there were no dances on, we went to see a lot of musicals at the cinema.

The musicals were *Meet Me in St Louis, Brazil, Lady, Let's Dance, Anchors Aweigh, Rhapsody in Blue*. We often heard the songs on the radio long before we saw the film, so we'd wind up singing along in the cinema.

Two of my favourites were 'Sentimental Journey' [Doris Day, 1945; it became the official homecoming song for US veterans] and 'Till the End of Time' [also 1945, sung by Perry Como and later Doris Day].

Many factories only had half-door toilets with a disc system. The time clerk gave you a disc and you got five minutes in the toilet – or else. Some of the gents' had a long open trough with water running through it, so a paper lit and dropped in at the end floated down the trough and then SCREAMS as the nether regions were seared. We sang loudly in those gents to let people know we were there.

The radio was all we had other than a wind-up gramophone and my piano and accordion.

On a Sunday afternoon we had tea and sang round the piano – it was the way we entertained ourselves in a time when we needed some relief from the toil and weariness of wartime. We were all good singers.

Throughout the war, the recorded voices of popular female singers were inspirational for millions everywhere, sometimes on the radio and in live performances to the troops across the world. Many of these wartime singers were American but the most beloved of all English 'Forces Sweethearts' were:

Vera Lynn (1917–2020) needs little introduction. Songs like 'We'll Meet Again' (from 1939) and 'The White Cliffs of Dover' (1942) remain the most popular recorded songs of the twentieth century. They are still popular.

Anne Shelton (1923–94) was just twelve when she launched her singing career on BBC Radio. Her most inspirational song was 'I'll Be Seeing You' (also recorded by Vera Lynn and many others). During the war, Churchill suggested Anne record 'Lili Marlene' (a huge German wartime hit) in English. Anne toured British military bases to entertain the troops. Her popularity soared post-war.

Gracie Fields (1898–1979) was enormously popular as a singer and actress throughout the 1930s. In 1939 she became seriously ill and moved to the island of Capri, Italy. Married to Monty Banks, an Italian citizen, Gracie became a highly controversial figure – as an Italian citizen Monty could have been interned in England after Italy entered the war in 1940.

At the suggestion of Winston Churchill – who reputedly told Gracie, 'Make American dollars, not British pounds' – Gracie and her husband moved to California, making occasional visits to the UK to perform in factories and Army camps. Later in the war she travelled to perform for Allied troops in New Guinea and at the end of the war to the Pacific Islands, relaunching her UK career in 1947 with BBC Radio.

Petula Clark was born in 1932 in Hook, near Kingston upon Thames. In 1942, aged ten, she started singing on BBC Radio and from there made some 500 BBC broadcasts, becoming the youngest of all of Britain's Forces Sweethearts with a postwar, hugely successful international career in music and films which resonates even today. Yet when World War II broke out she and her family moved from southern England to South Wales to live in a stone house without electricity, running water and an outside toilet.

Petula recalls: 'The Germans used to fly over us into London and it was pretty hectic. Mum was Welsh, so we'd go off to Wales which I loved.

'That was totally different, of course, No bombing where we were, near Merthyr, Abercanaid, Pentrebach. There was music everywhere. The first time I sang in public was in front of a congregation in the chapel. I was five or six, very shy, but somehow when I was singing I was able to shake off my shyness.

'There was that wonderful feeling of singing for people, and they were obviously enjoying it. That was it. I was hooked forever. Wales was important.'

## 'THE MOST DANGEROUS WOMAN IN EUROPE'

Britain's royal family nowadays are viewed as global mass entertainment, an ongoing historical saga-cum-soap opera. Yet attitudes to the royals, in Britain and its Commonwealth, were far more reverent in an era when class distinction was still a big part of everyday life.

As a result, on 8 May 1945, when King George VI, Queen Elizabeth and their daughters, Margaret and the then Princess Elizabeth, repeatedly stood on the balcony at Buckingham Palace alongside Churchill, (there were eight appearances) waving to an ecstatic crowd, the formal end of wartime underlined even greater popular respect for the royals. There were several reasons for this.

The royal family had remained in the country throughout, rejecting Churchill's plan in 1940 that they should move abroad in the event of German invasion. Though they decamped to the comparative safety of Windsor Castle, throughout the war the family had consistently shown themselves to the public as figureheads for the nation's morale, actively engaged in facing the troubled times alongside the British public, a symbol of resistance and British pride.

Not long after war broke out in October 1940, princesses Elizabeth and her sister Margaret Rose broadcast to the nation on the BBC Children's Hour, on behalf of the many children who had been evacuated from home, an early indication of the royal determination to use broadcasting as well as personal appearances to demonstrate their resolve.

A week into the Blitz, on 13 September 1940, a German bomber flew straight down The Mall to drop six bombs onto Buckingham Palace, one destroying the chapel. The bombs fell into a quadrangle just outside the sitting room where the King and Queen were seated. Afterwards, forty reporters were invited to view the damage, giving a sense, early on in the war, of a family determined to pull together with its people.

After the war, Winston Churchill wrote: 'Had the windows been closed ... the glass would have splintered into the faces of the King and Queen, causing terrible injuries.

So little did they make of it that even I, who saw them and their entourage so frequently, only realised long afterwards ... what actually happened.'

It was reported that the royals had adopted the austere routines of war, i.e. using ration books, ploughing up the royal estate at Sandringham as part of the Dig for Victory poster campaign (launched to encourage everyone to grow their own food in times of rationing).

They then closed the Sandringham estate, with the King and Queen using Windsor as a weekend retreat, though the two princesses used it as their home, learning how to operate a stirrup pump to douse incendiary bombs. (The official version was the princesses were based in a house 'somewhere in England'.)

Windsor Castle bristled with anti-aircraft guns as the German bombers droned overhead and air-raid shelters were installed in the castle courtyards. The Crown Jewels were wrapped in newspaper and stored in bomb-proof vaults.

During the autumn of 1940 the King and Queen toured the streets of London and other war-damaged cities in a packed schedule, travelling in the King's bulletproof car or on the royal train. This schedule of travelling the country to offer support continued during the war years with the King also travelling abroad widely. Munitions factories – where millions worked around the clock to produce the weapons of wartime – also received royal visits.

Security, of course, would have been a huge issue in newspaper or broadcast reporting of any detail, i.e. locations. So it was the unannounced public appearances at bomb-ravaged sites which gave the people the real sense that the royals were fully committed to their duty to support the nation. This pattern of royal events to support the nation continued long after VE Day.

At the age of nineteen the then Princess Elizabeth joined the ATS (Auxiliary Territorial Service), training as a driver and mechanic as a second subaltern, promoted to the equivalent of captain five months later – the only female of the royal family to enter the armed forces.

On 6 June, despite opposition, the King and Churchill came ashore on the Normandy beachhead. Even after the events of D-Day, the royals encountered another near-miss when a V-1 flying bomb fell on the Guards' Chapel, in Birdcage Walk, perilously close to Buckingham Palace, killing 121 soldiers and civilians.

The then Queen Elizabeth (The Queen Mother) with her warm smile, glamorous attire and unstinting dedication to supporting the nation became the epitome of the royal family's boost to the nation's morale.

In newsreels and photographs she shone vividly in proud defiance of the enemy. Towards the demise of Nazi Germany, Hitler was reputed to call her: 'The Most Dangerous Woman in Europe'.

## THE LOCAL HEROES

At the other end of the scale, Britain's civilian population comprised a huge wartime resource. Unpaid, they stepped forward voluntarily to 'do their bit'.

From the beginnings of the 'phoney war' in September 1939 to May 1940, the ARP wardens were mostly part-time wardens. Their job was essentially to organise the distribution of gas masks, check shelter provision and enforce blackout regulations.

When the Blitz started, their role took centre stage. Set up in ARP Control Posts and wearing tin hats they patrolled the local streets during a raid, checked out bomb shelters, reviewed the situation when a bomb fell, passed on messages and helped direct rescue operations by the heavy rescue squad, first aid groups, ambulances, demolition workers and, if needed, mortuary vans.

Set up to expand peacetime fire brigades, the AFS (Auxiliary Fire Service) listed 200,000 recruits when war broke out. The AFS volunteers were invaluable in helping fight fires caused by incendiary and high-explosive devices. The police force was also augmented by wartime volunteers.

The unofficial motto of the WVS (Women's Voluntary Service) was 'We Never Say No' and over 1 million women volunteering in virtually every aspect of wartime life got involved. It was the WVS that made such an important contribution in helping with the evacuation of thousands of urban children to the countryside. They also organised and ran mobile canteens around the country, helped with those who had been bombed out of their homes, stood as 'information points' at bomb incidents everywhere and got involved with a myriad of other wartime tasks. They provided essential back-up.

Fire-watching for incendiary bombs was compulsory for civilians at the end of 1940. Spotters stood on rooftops watching for planes, in order to let people carry on working until the bombers were nearly overhead. Then they'd immediately give the alarm.

Even children contributed as volunteers, carrying out a range of tasks: all part of civil defence. Margaret Haywood lived in the Orpington, Kent, area with her family. She was seventeen when she started to fire-watch.

I decided to fire-watch in order to 'do my bit' for the community. I used to watch from a neighbour's house which was on top of a hill. Three nights a week, I and another girl would go up and watch for the entire night. If we saw any fires we had to phone up the fire department to tell them. We weren't organised by any outside agency, we just wanted to get involved. In the day I'd work at Sevenoaks Cinema which stayed open during the war, and later on there were special screenings when the soldiers started to come back.

Thankfully we didn't see many fires but we did see enough to make you feel that what you were doing was important. We'd moved to Orpington from London just before the war started, so at first I felt a bit of an insider fire-watching, but after a while it was easy to get along because everybody pulled together.

# CHAPTER 4

# LOVE & ROMANCE

*'Everyone is getting married and engaged'*
DAILY EXPRESS, 1939

The war threw everyone into thinking quickly. 'Any girl who ends up in this war not married … is simply not trying' said the *Daily Express* at the time.

After war was declared in September 1939 many courting couples, unsure of the future, chose to marry before war separated them through conscription, evacuation or air raids. Marriage offered a sense of permanence and continuity – even if these things might never take place.

In 1940 there were 534,000 weddings, 40,000 more than the previous year in Britain.

Brides were younger too, with three out of every ten exchanging marriage vows being under twenty-one. Even before the long absences of men abroad started to take hold,

the hasty war nuptials peaked. Everything looked so dangerous ahead that careful thought seemed irrelevant – wait until
tomorrow and you could be dead. Seize the moment.

The wedding had a practical element too. Wives of
servicemen would be entitled to a marriage allowance. If
a husband was killed in action, they would be entitled to a
widow's pension.

My parents, Molly and Ginger, were part of the 1940
wedding surge. In 1939 they had been courting for six
years, but had never opted to get engaged. Ginger, I discovered decades later from the 1939 Register – a mini-census
of the time, taken as war broke out, giving the basic details
of the lives of 41 million people in the UK – was registered
as living with my mother's family at the time. The Register
described him as unemployed.

What I learned years later from my mother was that my
father was considering avoiding the call-up. He told Molly
he had been toying with desertion. As a typical East Ender
he knew many 'duckers and divers' who might give him a
few tips on how to get out of the call-up, and survive the war.

Molly's response, not surprisingly, was very clear.

'I'm not going to be a deserter's wife, Ging,' she told him.
'No way.'

That was it. My dad registered for call-up. Due to a
childhood eye injury he was unfit for combat, designated
for a desk job as a clerk in the Royal Army Pay Corps. He
wore this uniform on the photo of their wedding day in
June 1940 at Hackney Register Office. My mum sported an

eye-catching dotted dress with puffed sleeves, her sleek hair in a snood. She was almost twenty-four, a fashion-conscious shop assistant in London's Oxford Street. Her new RAPC husband was twenty-nine.

Was it a love match one might wonder? Not really. My dad had always been obsessively enamoured of my mother, even asking friends to 'keep an eye on Molly' when he took off travelling around the south of England in the pre-war days of his itinerant working life. My mum? When I asked her why, the response was always, 'Well … I felt sorry for Ging.' He'd had a tough, streetwise East End childhood, growing up in quite a different world to my mother's quieter, somewhat more genteel background, a big family with Russian emigrant parents headed by her father, a hard-working breadwinner.

Perhaps, in some ways, they weren't really well matched. But the sudden rush to matrimony meant there was no time to stop and reflect, or plan for life. All around them their peers were taking the plunge too. War was now. Tomorrow? No one knew.

This surge towards matrimony cut across all classes.

Winston Churchill's only son, Randolph (1911–68), was desperate to seize the moment. At twenty-nine he had been called up to the 4th Queen's Own Hussars a month before war was declared. Convinced he might die, a need for a Churchill heir was paramount in his thinking. He'd already tried to find a bride without success. Could a blind date rescue him?

A friend gave him a phone number. He called and enquired the name and appearance of the stranger. She was a nineteen-year-old from Dorset, and her father was the 11th Baron Digby.

'I'm Pamela Digby, red-haired and rather fat, but mummy says that puppy fat disappears,' she told him.

Puppy fat or otherwise, Randolph didn't hesitate. He proposed at the end of their first dinner in late September 1939. They married the following month and their only son, Winston Jnr, was born in October 1940. (Winston Jnr died in 2010.)

The wartime marriage to Pamela was turbulent: both had numerous affairs, though Pamela formed a strong bond with her father-in-law when he became prime minister in 1940.

The couple divorced in 1946. Pamela subsequently remarried, first to US Democrat diplomat Averell Harriman and later to Broadway producer Leland Hayward. She died in 1997, a glittering socialite with a very high profile track record. Randolph's second marriage to June Osborne in 1948 ended in divorce in 1961. The war also turned class or status differences upside down. At times it placed people from very different backgrounds close together, resulting in all manner of friendships, love affairs and marriages. Romance would blossom very quickly and time together would become far more precious – or urgent – than it ever had in peacetime.

## 'DEEP DOWN, INSTINCT TOLD ME WE WOULDN'T HAVE LONG TOGETHER'

Yvonne Gough-Macdonald (1921–2015) grew up in Cirencester, Gloucestershire. She was eighteen when war broke out and had recently started teaching at a local primary school.

At that point I was going out with my first boyfriend, Peter, a boy I'd known at school. Cirencester started to be surrounded by aircraft bases as they were building them all over the south of England, so we were at the heart of things.

Peter signed up for the RAF just after he'd turned eighteen. He was more of a good friend; I wasn't expecting to marry him. He was killed at nineteen; went down over the Channel during the Battle of Britain in September 1940. So many young men my sister and I met during those early war years didn't make it. We were all so unformed.

And innocent.

It was still a relatively quiet life. Most of the fighting was on the south coast. I can remember a plane that was shot down not far from Cirencester; that was a big excitement. We didn't get as much of the bombing as some other parts of the country.

I met Tom Wheatley in the summer of 1940, just before I turned nineteen. There was a local swimming pool that was very popular with anyone in uniform, and I met him there.

Then he was posted near Aylesbury in Buckinghamshire. He was nineteen, an acting pilot officer in the RAF.

Tom was so sophisticated compared to the Cirencester boys I knew. He'd been to Dulwich Prep School. He came from Kent and he had a car. His stepfather was a colonel in the Queen's Regiment. He'd travelled.

Tom came from a very different world. On one of our early dates he took me out for dinner to a lovely inn, the Swan at Bibury, one of the nicest places to eat in the area. I was a little bit nervous. I was still in awe of him, so different to the local boys. While we were eating, Tom discovered something crawling on a piece of lettuce. He just flicked it off the leaf with his fork. To a young, innocent country girl, it seemed so clever, knowing how to handle something like that. I was impressed with his sophistication. And smitten.

I kept on seeing him through that summer of 1940. A couple of times I travelled to his base and stayed in a hotel nearby on the main street. Then we'd go out at night. I didn't ask my mother if it was OK to go, which was unusual for me. I just wanted to be with Tom. In those days it was tough having young daughters. There were so many of those attractive young men in uniform around the area. I continued to teach and we'd meet up whenever we could. Or we'd write to each other. It was constant movement for Tom. He was training so he was sent up to Yorkshire at some stage, and by then he was learning to fly heavy bombers.

I thought I was in love with Tom, but I suppose I was a bit of a camp follower as far as he was concerned. We travelled around together whenever we could manage it that summer of 1941.

Something told me, as young as I was, that I had to spend as much time as possible with him. Deep down, instinct told me we wouldn't have very long together. I did go out with other boys, briefly. But after less than eighteen months of seeing each other, we married in February 1942.

There was no proposal as such. It was more like, "Why don't you marry me and travel with me?" Something casually slipped into the conversation. There was no going down on one knee, that sort of stuff. Life was going too fast.

We all knew we didn't have time to obey the rules. The war itself made you hurry. Better to make a decision and do something because tomorrow it might be gone.

It was a strange time for decision-making. In a way, you didn't really think you'd be spending your life with someone. Not when all around you, people you knew, were being killed. At one point I'd gone to see a boy I knew at his base, only to be told he'd had an accident and been killed. The whole thing made you feel as if the ground was constantly shifting under your feet.

We married in the lovely, big St John Baptist Church in Cirencester's market square. Tom's mother and aunt came up from Kent but his stepfather was away fighting in the Middle East. Tom's mother had divorced his real father when Tom was two and remarried. Tom had been born in America, then brought back to Kent.

My parents were a bit nervous about meeting Tom's mother, Nan. It was a very small wedding. I wore a pale green suit with a spray of green and brown orchids. There was no time for a proper honeymoon, so we just stayed at a local inn. We only had a few days together. Then he had to go back to his base and I had to go back home because I was still teaching.

There were no married quarters for us on his base as newlyweds. During the war you couldn't have wives on the base because some of the bases were very dangerous places to be. So when he was moved around from base to base we'd have to find different 'homes' for ourselves. After we married I'd left my teaching job. I don't think I slept away from Tom the entire time we were married.

When he had a new posting we'd drive to the new area in Tom's 1930s car, a yellow Renault. We'd put my bike on the jump seat at the back; then we'd find a suitable village and split up. He'd go to the base and I'd get on the bike, go round the village and knock on doors to see if someone would rent a room to us in their house.

We'd pay about £2 a week for the room. By the time we met up that evening I'd usually have found someone to take us in. There were lots of these opportunities during the war, but mostly you'd only be staying in the house for a couple of months. The money was always welcome.

It was always ordinary, working-class people who took us in. One woman hated us having a bath, because she didn't like her bathroom being messed up. But people were kind.

Once, Tom was posted up to Scotland. We found a room in a house where a brother and sister lived, running a grocery store together.

When Tom was posted to a base in Leeming, south of York, early in 1943, you could hear the planes because we were so close to the base. In March he went off on his first big bombing raid in a Halifax bomber. On that trip he was second pilot.

The trip was for practice, his first-ever trip over Berlin. He'd done some small trips with his own crew but this was a big one.

After he'd gone off on the flight the people we were staying with were so kind. They suggested we play cards. Anything to distract me from the sound of all the planes going over until I went to bed.

That morning, there was an unexpected knock on the door. Two people, a minister and a woman volunteer, both from Tom's base. I knew it was my turn as soon as I saw them. Tom hadn't come back.

The first thing I did was call Tom's mother, Nan. She'd just lost her son. But she'd also lost her husband six months before. Nan said she'd meet me at the station at York and we could then go back to her home in Kent together.

Nan's first words to me when we met were: 'I can be brave if you can.'

That first night, she slept in the bed with me, the same bed her son had slept in the night before he was killed. The next day we drove back to her house in Chislehurst, Kent, and I stayed there.

About three months later a telegram arrived for me. It was from the King. Tom's body had been buried in Antwerp, Belgium. His plane had been brought down by a German fighter plane over Holland on the border with Belgium. Tom and one other fellow went down with the plane. When the Germans picked up their bodies, they took them across to Belgium.

Determined to do something for the war effort, Yvonne trained as a ferry pilot for the Air Transport Auxiliary, delivering different types of planes from the factory to RAF airfields until the war ended. In May 1945 she remarried to Neil Macdonald, a flyer from the Royal Canadian Air Force. The couple went to live in Canada, raising five children, a happy and successful marriage. Neil died in 2001.

As she said later: 'The whole experience of the war made a lot of difference to the way I turned out; it put steel in the backbone. Once you've come through something like flying in wartime and losing a husband at such a young age, nothing can get you down very much.'

Losing a husband after a brief young marriage was sadly a frequent aspect of World War II. Yet Yvonne's story of remaking her life after the tragedy of loss was not very unusual. But it was also well known that war created the rupture of existing relationships or even marriages which fell apart due to separation – and years apart in very different environments.

## 'I LOST MY WARTIME GIRLFRIEND
## – AND FOUND TRUE LOVE'

This is exactly what happened to Roy Pryor from Ashford, Kent. Roy, twenty-five, a corporal with the RAMC (Royal Army Medical Corps) had been captured in France at the time of Dunkirk in 1940. He had spent four very difficult years as a POW in Poland, Czechoslovakia and Germany when he was finally repatriated (for health reasons) in the summer of 1944 (See Chapter 5).

Waiting for him amongst the excited crowd at the station to greet him were his family and his long-term girlfriend Dorothy, whom he'd known since he was a teenager.

It was a red-letter day for everyone. It was like time had stood still, getting back home to my old bedroom with all the photos of film stars on the wall. After I came back, I went on a training course for three months; they promised I could be posted near home for six months. Yet on the course I felt restless, I wanted to DO something. A new trade had been created in the RAMC for people like me, which was to provide support for hospital consultants. It meant three months of learning medical terms and shorthand.

One day they sent me to Sevenoaks for a few months to relieve a girl who was having difficulty with her shorthand. At Sevenoaks there was a very social atmosphere; we all celebrated VE Day there. As for my girlfriend Dorothy, she seemed more interested in what other people were doing. She was very much part of the Ashford Youth Club and regarded herself as a bit of an auntie to the boys. A lot of them were sweet on Dorothy but as for me, I had little in common with those boys. I still had this restlessness – and I seemed to have moved on somehow with her. I found her conversation boring. We were just drifting apart.

After Christmas I was moved to fill in for a clerk who was on compassionate leave in Catterick, North Yorkshire. I'd been there for about a fortnight when this VAD (this was the Voluntary Aid Detachment, providing nursing care for military personnel) Pat Burns, came back from leave.

While I'd been filling in for her I had heard, 'Oh, you've not met Burns.' And when I did ... she was everything I wanted in a woman. I have never forgotten that moment. I was laying the fire in the office early in the morning when she walked in. Tiny, very pretty, very feminine, ladylike.

I quickly found she was feisty too. Her sense of fair play was exactly the same as mine when it came to caring for other people. As we worked together that morning, everything gelled. By the next day, I was in love. It was that quick.

The next time I had some leave I was due to meet up with an old friend but I didn't want to go. I told Pat I wanted to go out with her instead, a meal to say goodbye because I was supposed to go back to York.

But I had no intention of saying goodbye to her. I wanted to see her the next weekend. So I arranged a B & B for her in York and that weekend we went to the theatre; it was *Emma* by Jane Austen.

Pat was nineteen, I was twenty-six. We could see each other each weekend but it wasn't enough.

We'd meet in Darlington on Wednesday night for a meal. This went on for a few weeks. Then, out of the blue, an order came through: Pat was going to be posted to a new unit being set up in Oxford. She was being transferred away from me. We always suspected that this was the work of her family. Her father was a major in the RAMC and was very protective of her. I took her down to Oxford and we arranged to meet up the following weekend at London's Paddington station. We snatched time to see each other, sometimes just for a few hours, in London or Oxford, for the next year.

By Easter 1946, Pat's family had finally given me the seal of approval. As for Dorothy, we'd never actually said,

"Let's finish it." It had just fizzled out in those earlier months when I'd still been in the south of England.

We could have waited a year until Pat was twenty-one but in the end we were married in Salisbury on 22 March 1947. We had our honeymoon, one night at the Strand Palace Hotel in London, and drove away to our life together in our little Morris 8.

[Note: Roy and Pat lived happily together for seventy years, many as a retired couple in rural France, until Roy's death at the age of ninety-six in July 2016. Dorothy was godmother to their first child, daughter Jill.]

When it came to organising a wartime wedding, normal plans would be fraught with dilemmas and difficulties. Transport was a big issue: would the wedding couple or guests be able to use transport to get there on time? Getting around was complicated. Railway schedules were frequently thrown into disarray. For those with a car, rationing meant petrol shortages; nothing could be taken for granted. As for the groom and best man already in the Forces, getting leave might be tricky: could they get leave at precisely the right time?

Civilians too had the same problem when wanting to get time off work. Even if there was a forty-eight-hour leave pass, would a couple need to obtain a special licence? What about the honeymoon? Would there be enough time to get away? Or would it have to be postponed indefinitely? Even the timing of the ceremony could be difficult: with city-based couples it wasn't unusual to get married during an air raid.

Ron Axford from Bristol was a gunner and driver mechanic with the Army. It looked like he would be sent abroad to fight in Europe so he decided to get permission to marry from his colonel who gave him forty-eight hours' home leave for the occasion. Ron and his bride-to-be, Muriel, were both under twenty-one so needed their parents' permission to marry. Ron remembered:

It was all arranged so quickly. The wedding preparations had to be speeded up. Muriel made all the arrangements for the marriage licence, wedding ring and a car to take us to church. A wedding car was governed by distance, petrol consumed and a time limit of two hours. Muriel was so relieved when someone she knew managed to get a film for their camera to record the big event.

By this time in 1944, everyone was feeling the pinch. Family and friends all chipped in for the clothing coupons for the wedding dress. Muriel managed to purchase a length of white velvet for the wedding dress, buy two dresses for her bridesmaids and include sufficient material to make into little suits for the two pageboys. Her mother had to conjure them up so quickly her feet hardly left the heavy treadle of the sewing machine she kept under the stairs.

When the two families got together to make a list of wedding guests it surprised them – seventy-six! Far more than they were expected to feed, even for a wedding. The only thing allowed on ration was two pounds of cooked ham – nothing more. Family and friends donated rations of butter, tea and sugar; some gave up their precious bottles of preserves and the men raided their winter stores of potatoes, beetroot, swede and prized hothouse salads. My sister offered a wedding cake using what ingredients had been donated and it was put on display – with all the trimmings she could find.

An uncle with some know-how managed to get his hands on a leg of lamb. No questions asked and it was hastily cooked in the bride's mother's coal-fired oven and with some of her chicken's eggs, hard-boiled. It was beginning to look as if a wedding feast was imminent.

My mother extracted a promise of red roses from a local florist in Bristol for the bride's bouquet. A dozen were produced on the day – an entire month's ration for the florist.

As things were hotting up, Muriel began to worry that I might not turn up on time for my wedding. Rumours were always circulating about sudden postings. This could happen. By 10pm on the day before the wedding it began to look like her fears were about to be realised; she was going up the wall worrying if the groom was going to make it.

I was due to arrive at 6pm on Friday night at Bristol Temple Meads railway station.

What the bride didn't realise was that there was no public transport to get me from Bristol to the village of Frampton Cotterell in the blackout. The only choice was to walk the eight miles through the empty roads and lanes in the dark. A policeman stopped me on the way and asked what I was doing on my own at night. I told him I was on leave and about to get married the next day, but I was worried that I might be asked to empty my kitbag – my service revolver was at the bottom. It didn't happen and I reached the bride's house at 10pm.

My parents also lived in Bristol. In their wedding clothes there was no other way to get to the village but by bus on the day.

Our wedding took place at the Hebron Methodist Church in Coalpit Heath, just east of Frampton Cotterell. We had two bridesmaids and two young pages in attendance. Muriel's younger brother Ian was an usher at the church. One of the pages asked him what he had to do when the bride and groom got to the front of the church.

Being something of a joker he whispered loudly: 'Get hold of the bride's veil and give it a tug.' We heard him and gave him a very dirty look. The other pageboy spent the entire prayer time when I was on my knees touching every one of the steel studs in the bottom of my shoes, counting them with his finger.

But all went well and the wedding feast was enough for the guests. Muriel wondered what her mother had been up to when she caught her sneaking downstairs with one of the sleeves of her dress covered in white powder. After all the guests had departed, Muriel and I found ourselves up to our elbows in washing-up until 1.30am.

When we finally got upstairs to our wedding bed and pulled back the top sheet, we knew what her mother had been up to. Muriel pulled the sheet covered in flour off the bed; exhausted, the newly marrieds were content to sleep on the bare mattress.

We got ten teapots as wedding presents. I was back in barracks the following day by 9pm. Still wearing my Army uniform.

For a bride, of course, there was the big question of the wedding dress; much easier for those in the Forces to choose to wear military uniform. (Women serving in the WRNS, the WAAF or the ATS, often did so.) Some brides wore smart day clothes and brightened the outfit with a jaunty hat. Others would simply borrow a wedding dress from a relative or neighbour.

At the start of the war it was considered unpatriotic to have a big, flashy wedding. Later it changed: having a wedding as near normal as possible was considered the best way. Overall, rationing of food and clothing tended to dominate the decisions of the wartime bride. A lot of brides opted to make their own dresses, using curtains, tablecloths and, if they were lucky enough to source one, a salvaged silk parachute.

It was possible to hire a wedding dress. Eleanor Roosevelt, the wife of the wartime American president, had collected a number of pre-war wedding dresses which she hired out to British service brides.

Dame Barbara Cartland (1901–2000), then a commander in the ATS (Auxiliary Territorial Service), firmly believed that service brides should marry in style. She managed to purchase over 120 bridal dresses, and these could be hired by any servicewoman for just about £1.

Even the smaller details like the ring were difficult. Gold had become very scarce. The government permitted the manufacture of 'utility' wedding rings in nine-carat gold, instead of the usual twenty-two carat. Yet there were never enough rings like this to meet demand; many had to search second-hand shops for their wedding rings.

As for confetti, it was illegal to make it, so canny office workers would save little discs of paper from hole punches to use as confetti.

Feeding guests also required a great deal of ingenuity. Extra coupons could be obtained from the Food Office for a permit for a wedding party for up to forty guests but the amounts permitted were very small. In July 1940, the making or selling of iced cakes was forbidden. Luxuries were unavailable. Spam and dried egg sandwiches tended to be the usual wedding fare. Families would improvise with whatever they could source to create something festive.

In some wartime wedding photos the cake is often seen as a traditional three-tiered luxury cake. This was usually an illusion. Bakers would hire out cardboard covers to place over whatever modest cake was on offer (normally a sponge made with dried eggs).

## 'PORK SALAD AND A CAKE WITH REAL ICING, FOOD YOU HADN'T SEEN FOR YEARS'

Ivy Gardiner (1924–2019) was a munitions worker in World War II on the Wirral, near Liverpool, living through the devastating Liverpool Blitz of 1940–1.

Ivy lived in the Wirral area for her entire life. In 2012 she was awarded an MBE for her long-term dedication to the Brownie movement.

I turned twenty-one not long after D-Day. We knew that was the real turning point. I'll never forget my birthday gift from my mother: just one tiny chocolate éclair. She had stood in a queue for an hour to buy it.

I'd been courting my boyfriend, Wilf, since war broke out. Wilf was from an Army family, but his brothers all went into the Navy. Wilf wound up in a reserved job because he had a hearing problem, so he was a fitter and turner for the Navy – eventually he was making rum barrels for the Navy in Birkenhead.

We'd go to the pictures whenever we could. One unforgettable night was the time Wilf and I were sitting watching a film in the Ritz Cinema, Birkenhead. It was December 1940 and the sirens went off.

I jumped up immediately: 'I'm going, Wilf!'

He was a bit unsure, wanting to watch the rest of the film. But common sense told him to come out after me. As we walked along the road you could see the planes above, getting ready to drop their bombs. And they did come down, straight onto the roof of the Ritz, killing ten people and injuring a hundred – exactly where we'd been sitting.

Of course we were all desperate for it to be over and for us to win the war. The propaganda was wonderful: 'Be like Dad, Keep Mum' they told us. Nobody ever thought we would lose.

New Year 1945 and my munitions work stopped. Then I went back to normal factory work. Just after VE Day on 25 May, Wilf and I had our wedding.

But it was hardship. Spam salad for a wedding reception. My mum and Wilf's mum got together, as you couldn't get things like icing easily. So Mum swapped all her coupons to get all her friends to look out for icing.

In the end I had a three-tier cake. With real icing. And all the swapping meant we got a quarter of a pig. It was wonderful. Pork salad and a big cake with real icing. You hadn't seen things like that for ages.

All my friends got married in borrowed white dresses. In the end I bought a blue silk coat in Liverpool and a hat with ostrich feather and veiling. As a wedding present, my mother managed to buy us a ticket to fly to the Isle of Man. I think it would have been one of the first planes to leave Liverpool airport after the war. When you looked out of the window you could see all the guns along Liverpool Bay, a reminder of all we'd gone through.

Wilf and I were virgins when we married; neither of us had a clue what to do.

No one told you in those days. We went to live with Wilf's mother in North Birkenhead and we stayed with her for five years until my daughter Lynn arrived. Then we managed to get a council house.

Really, the authorities only told us what they wanted us to know. But as soon as we'd been told about D-Day, we knew the war was going our way.

## 'EVERYONE CHIPPED IN'

Frank Mee from Stockton-on-Tees recalled how a wedding in his village frequently became a joint effort.

We always knew when the local regiments were on the move by the flood of weddings. Mum, as a tailoress, would alter dresses for the girls, taking off the trimmings and putting on new ones from some other dress that had not been used so often. She always managed to make them look different – which pleased the bride.

We always gave something towards the wedding break-fast: bacon, ham, vegetables from the garden, all sorts of goodies came out of secret stores and sometimes the lads managed to get tins of meat or sugar and tea from the mess when the cooks knew a wedding was on the cards. Everyone in the village would attend the church and give them a send-off. We lads would close the churchyard gates until the groom would throw handfuls of pennies and then as we scattered to pick them up they would escape.

It usually became a walk across the green for a photo if there was any film around.

On one very memorable occasion my dad decked his truck out and put a seat on the back. The bride and groom climbed a short ladder to the back and then sat as he drove slowly up and down the village to cheers. Or a car would be provided from one of the better-off villagers.

On the day the women of the village would deck the place out for the reception. They would lay out the food, make the tea and serve up – under the orders of the bride's mother between her tears – and it would be an all-round success right down to the family fight after the bride and groom retired. Fisticuffs on the green often enough after a wedding – we'd expect it as part of the show!

Once married, couples were often separated by war for years – even finding a home together once war ended would prove difficult – and lengthy.

## 'HE TURNED UP AT MY HOUSE. WE WERE MARRIED THREE WEEKS LATER.'

Vera Barber was born in 1924. She has lived all her life in Bishop Auckland, County Durham, and has been married to her husband, Philip, since 1945. They have one son, Gary. During the war Vera worked in the offices of the vast Aycliffe munitions factory in Aycliffe, a factory which had opened in 1941.

I met Philip in 1939 in the grounds of Auckland Castle. I'd gone out walking with a friend; it was a Sunday afternoon. I was nearly fifteen. I was wearing a coat with a pocket where I'd put my hanky in, but for some reason the hanky dropped to the ground. Philip was out walking with his friend just behind us.

He was the same age as me and already in the Army, as a trumpeter. He came from Mablethorpe in Lincolnshire but he'd been sent to Bishop Auckland by his regiment, the 52nd Anti-Tank Regiment.

Philip spotted my hanky, picked it up and handed it to me. Naturally, we got talking. Then he asked me out, to the pictures.

'No,' I said. 'I'll be going to church.' But I did agree to meet up with him another time.

He was very smart in his uniform, I liked him immediately. After that first meeting we started seeing each other for about a year.

But the war was on and for some reason we had a bit of a falling-out. It was something daft – but we stopped seeing each other.

I didn't know it but he had moved into maritime artillery. He was on board ship.

In 1945, as the war was drawing to a close, I got a letter from Philip's mother to say his vessel had been torpedoed. Philip was seriously ill in Simon's Town, South Africa. Would I write to him? 'He's still asking after you, Vera,' she said.

I'd had other boyfriends in the interim. But I thought it was right that I should write to him, so I did. And we kept on writing, right until the day he came back to Bishop Auckland.

I didn't realise it until afterwards but he'd headed straight for my house, instead of his home in Mablethorpe.

He knew where I lived. One day, he just turned up at the door. I knew he was serious about getting married because of all our letters. He proposed straight away. We were married in three weeks' time.

We managed to get a decent cake because my brother was stationed in India and he had sent home a big parcel of dried fruit, which we could use in a one-tier wedding cake.

We were married by special licence, and I'd just turned twenty-one when we married on 21 November 1945.

Phil had turned twenty-one on 30 April, so just six months older. I'd already stopped work at the Aycliffe munitions factory at the end of August.

I wasn't married in white but I was able to go and buy a nice pale green dress in a shop called Jones in Bishop, carrying just a spray of flowers.

For our honeymoon we went to stay with an aunt and uncle in Bedlington in Northumberland, just for a week.

We didn't set up home together as I was still living with my parents and Phil was still in the Army so he had to go back to Germany after the honeymoon.

Phil was a regular soldier, not a wartime soldier, so he remained in Germany for a few years, coming back on leave whenever permitted.

I found an office job, clerical work with a firm who had a shop in Darlington.

Our son, Gary, was born in January 1947. Philip was still in Germany when he was born but he got leave – so Gary was ten days old when his dad first saw him.

Gary was five years old when Philip finally came home in 1952. But we'd managed to get a house, a prefab I moved into in 1947 when Gary was six months old.

I lived on my own with Gary until Philip came back and we wound up staying in the prefab for nine years. I loved the prefab: you had a built-in cupboard for everything – they were lovely houses. Then we moved to a council house and Phil went into factory work.

We didn't have a lot in those years before he left the Army – just Army allowance – and I didn't work again until Gary was fifteen. Wives stayed at home in those days.

How did everyone feel? People were just happy that the war was over. We just got on with life.

## THE GI GLAMOUR BOYS

America entered the war at the end of 1941, following the Japanese bombing of Pearl Harbor. Consequently, the arrival of the first of 1,500,000 American servicemen into Britain in January 1942 was both a momentous turning point in boosting the Allied cause towards victory – and into the lives of many young women.

The war brought servicemen to Britain from a host of other nations, amongst them French, Norwegian, Polish, Belgian, Dutch, Czech as well as former Commonwealth servicemen from Australia, New Zealand, Canada, India and South Africa but it was the Americans, most of all, who exuded a certain kind of glamour to drab, war-torn Britain.

Well dressed, often charming, polite – and earning five times as much as the average British serviceman – off-duty servicemen poured into London, the cities and the areas near their bases. At dance halls and gatherings all over the country, thousands of young women met them for the first time – and found themselves caught up in what was then dubbed 'GI fever'.

## 'GOT ANY GUM, CHUM?'

Alan Ladbrooke remembers the 1945 fascination of the GI – and their behaviour.

Chewing gum seemed exotic – chewing was what hard men and dubious women did in the American films we saw at the local cinema in the 1940s. It was also what American servicemen did as they strolled around the East Anglian town in which I was brought up.

Off duty, they walked the streets in their sleek uniforms, usually with a girl on their arm, chewing and feeling on top of the world, especially as the war had just finished.

There was something magnetic about them. It wasn't just their accents, nor was it the fact that they came from the very place we knew from the films, a place where everyone lived in skyscrapers amongst gangsters or in a mansion with flashy cars in the drive. The servicemen were important to us children, not because of the skyscrapers and cars, but because they had chewing gum.

With rationing during the war and the following years, the supply of sweets was limited. As children, we could get liquorice roots to chew, and we dipped rhubarb sticks into sugar to make them sweet but they weren't like the real thing. Certainly they couldn't compare with the gum that moved so rhythmically in the mouths of the Americans as they sauntered through our streets.

We had to have some.

So the catchphrase developed. The thing to do was to run up to an American, smile, and say: 'Got any gum, chum?'

It was always best if they had a girlfriend with them – they wouldn't refuse for fear of appearing mean. Usually they laughed and handed over a packet of the treasured stuff with a 'Sure, pal.'

It was a time of austerity. Austerity meant shortages, but often it brought out the best in people. While many might have envied visiting servicemen, it certainly encouraged everyone to be resourceful – especially as far as food was concerned.

'Got any gum, chum?' is a piece of personal history I share with my generation – who couldn't resist the attraction of making your mouth move in the way mouths did in the pictures.

In London's Piccadilly, the GI epicentre was an American Red Cross club called Rainbow Corner, on the corner of Denman Street, a hub for American servicemen, open round the clock, a slice of American 'all you can eat or drink' culture dished up far from home. At war's ending, Rainbow Corner even hosted special talks for English war brides who were about to marry these handsome strangers – and leave Britain for good.

Joy Beaver was born in 1925. She lived with her family in Bexleyheath, Kent. She wasn't a visitor to Rainbow Corner but at a local dance hall in September 1944, nineteen-year-old Joy was introduced to Army Corporal Carl Beebe, a handsome GI serving in the 6811th Signal Corps, working as an intercept officer.

I wanted to get on the dance floor but Carl said sorry, he didn't dance. Preferring to find someone who did dance, I just walked away. But he kept coming back to me. Then he asked if I would go for a walk with him and he walked me home. That was how it all started. Eight months later we got married in the final days of the war: Carl wore his Army uniform and I wore a wedding dress.

I'm not sure I thought too deeply about it at the time. I knew I wanted to marry Carl and that he felt the same way. We loved each other, though my mother had lots of doubts. But she liked him and so did the rest of my family. He had endeared himself to all of us. A visit from him was always a pleasure.

We had been bombed repeatedly by German aircraft and were at the mercy of V-1 (doodlebugs) and V-2 rockets. Our home had been badly damaged and homes of friends and neighbours had been destroyed.

Some of our neighbours had been killed. My father had died in 1941. He'd been gassed in World War I and in ill health for most of his life. My brother Tony, in the Marines, had a leg injury during parachute training and that caused him difficulty walking.

My grandmother had been evacuated to the country to be safe from air raids. My Auntie Alice's office around St Paul's Cathedral – where she worked for fifty years – had burned to the ground during a three-day incendiary raid by the Luftwaffe. Though others had far worse tragedies, we all wondered what else the future would hold. But getting married was a happy and exciting event to plan for.

My brother Tony managed to find me a wedding dress and veil on the black market. I kept the dress but I had to return the veil. My mother made the brides-maid's dresses. A mother of Tony's friend made me a proper wedding cake, a fruit cake with hard icing. This was probably another black market deal since eggs, dried fruits, butter, flour and sugar were rationed. Ma ordered a hire car to take me back and forth to the church and the reception was held in our front room for family and a few friends. It was only the third or fourth time I had even ridden in a car.

Our wedding on 28 April 1945 was at St John's Church, Welling. It had been badly damaged in air raids and it had a leaky roof; the stained-glass windows were shattered and boarded with wood.

It snowed that day as we walked into the church. Tony walked me down the aisle, though his shoulders were snow-covered. But when we came out the sun was bright and we had some good pictures taken by one of Carl's Army buddies, me in my wedding dress, Carl in his uniform.

Afterwards Carl and I took off on the train for the weekend to Arundel, Sussex.

The country hotel where we stayed served more fancy food than we had seen at home for years. Roast duck for dinner the first night! Carl and I had a good time walking and exploring the area, visiting an old castle, enjoying being together and not thinking about the war or any of its consequences. He didn't get any more leave until ten days later and on 8 May we set off to spend a week in a bed and breakfast in Worthing on the south coast.

So great was our excitement we paid very little attention to the news. When we started our journey to Worthing we found that practically the whole country had the day off to celebrate VE Day. What should have been a three-hour train trip took us all day. It was all part of our adventure together and we had a lovely week by the seaside.

It's hard to overstate how prevalent this phenomenon was. Between 1942 and 1952, one million women from over fifty countries married Americans. Of these an estimated 60,000–70,000 left the UK to emigrate to the US; 7,000 also left the UK to emigrate to Australia and New Zealand (3,700 women from 37 countries married New Zealand World War II servicemen).

## 'HE DID EVERYTHING HE COULD TO MAKE ME HAPPY.'

In 1946, Sylvia Smith left her friends and family behind to join her new husband, New Zealand flyer Leicester Smith, one of thousands of British women who emigrated to New Zealand in what were then called 'bride ships' in order to be with their servicemen husbands. (These women were known in New Zealand as 'Mr Jones' wives', named after the then Minister of Defence, Fred Jones, who oversaw the women's immigration.)

Sylvia, twenty, had met Leicester, twenty-five, in 1944 on a railway platform in Derby. At the time, the handsome New Zealander was based at RAF Upavon, Wiltshire as a flying instructor. As soon as she met the RNZAF pilot, Sylvia knew immediately that he was the one.

I had the funniest feeling, I thought, 'This is it, this is my destiny.' He thought the same thing; we both knew instantly. We wanted to get married straight away.

My father said: 'I'll do anything for Kiwis, they looked after me at Gallipoli in the [First World] war.'

But my mother said: 'Wait until your tour of duty over Germany has finished.

I don't want my daughter a widow.'

She had a point. In fact, Sylvia came perilously close to losing her husband-to-be. Not long after they met, Leicester was flying a Mosquito bomber over Holland when it collided with another Mosquito.

Leicester's plane went into a spin, diving 16,000 feet in seconds. He managed to straighten the plane out, release his bomb onto farmland and nurse the plane, with engine on fire, back to England. For his heroism he was awarded the DFC (Distinguished Flying Cross) in July 1945.

Sylvia and Leicester tied the knot as the war ended on 1 May 1945. It was a white wedding – thanks to Leicester's clothing coupons. As flight lieutenant he was entitled to receive eighty clothing coupons a year. (Civilians only got twenty-two.)

'Leicester always said I married him for his clothing coupons,' said Sylvia.

In September 1945, Leicester's former employers invited him to attend a year-long training course in the US; this would enable him to return to civilian life in New Zealand on a higher salary.

For Sylvia, however, this meant immediate separation – followed by a long wait to emigrate to New Zealand to be with her new husband.

Her fare on the 'bride ship' would be paid by the New Zealand government. But it would take several frustrating months before the formalities for emigration were arranged to send 400 war brides to Australia and 400 to New Zealand, many with children in tow, on board ship.

Finally, the ship, the *Athlone Castle*, set sail. Days passed slowly over the five-week voyage. Sylvia organised variety concerts which cheered everyone up. The *Athlone Castle* sailed into Wellington Harbour on Anzac Day, 25 April 1946. Yet even then, there was a frustrating delay.

'The wharfies (trade unions) wouldn't bring the ship in because it was a public holiday, so we had to wait for twenty-four hours,' recalls Sylvia.

When they finally disembarked, Sylvia spotted her father-in-law, waiting to drive her to her in-laws' home in Rangiora on New Zealand's South Island.

'Leicester had said I'd find it difficult in Rangiora – and I did, it was a small market town – and that was it.'

After a few months, Leicester arrived. He had a manager's job in Auckland. Finally they left Rangiora to head for the city of Auckland and start married life.

Yet it was very difficult at first. They struggled to find anywhere to live. For some reason, the new English brides were not warmly received. 'I said to Leicester, I've had enough, we're going home.'

But bit by bit things improved. At first the couple found a room in a house divided into self-contained flats, then Sylvia started working, first in a department store, then managing a vegetable stand in the city's markets. Very gradually life improved. When one of the adjacent flats in the house was vacated, the couple were ready to buy it – and remained living there for many years.

In the early 1950s the pair returned to England for a period of time but returned to New Zealand. Only then did Sylvia finally feel settled. The couple had two children and, over time, eight grandchildren. Theirs was a happy, contented life.

Later, Sylvia would recall that she was happy she made such a good choice of husband.

'Leicester knew he'd taken me away from everything I knew so he did everything he could to make me happy – the best husband anyone could ever have.'

The couple were married for sixty-seven years. Leicester died in July 2012, aged ninety-three. Sylvia died in December 2019, aged ninety-five.

## 'A BAD START TO A WEDDING DAY'

Hilda Tidball (1923–2014) grew up in Birmingham. Even as an eight-year-old she knew she'd fallen for her husband-to-be.

I was visiting my grandparents who lived in Shepton Mallet, Somerset. Alan lived in the same street. I next

met him in 1937 when I was staying with my grandmother again. Then in Christmas 1939 I was visiting
Shepton Mallet with my cousin. We spotted Alan and
a friend in the town, Alan looking so handsome in his
RAF uniform. We talked and walked together to the
park as a foursome. It was a moonlit night, very cold and
frosty, and we talked and exchanged addresses.

Back in Birmingham I got a letter one day, addressed
from LAC A R Tidball from Lyme Regis. Alan was in
the Marine Craft section of the RAF. I was so excited to
get that letter and we continued to write to each other.

In January 1940 Alan was invited to our home in
Saltley, Birmingham, to meet my parents. After that,
he'd come on the occasional weekend whenever he was
on leave.

Things were strict in those days. Sometimes we sat
together in an air-raid shelter and I used to pretend to
manicure his fingernails, just so we could hold each
other's hands. Finally we got engaged.

We were married at St Margaret's Church in Ward
End, Saltley, on 3 August 1942. Arranging our wedding
was no easy matter. In Birmingham we had lots of bombings and supplies of everything were short, particularly
food and fuel. I would stand at Saltley gas station from
6am until I was served.

One time my mother and I were pushing a pram
carrying a large galvanised tub full of water. We had
fetched it from Duddeston Mill. It was a long walk to

where we lived and all uphill. When we got to Saltley Gate the policeman had to stop the traffic.

The wheel had come off the pram and we were in danger of losing all our precious water. But we had help to get the pram and the water back to safety.

I was nineteen and Alan twenty-one. Couples generally married younger at that time. You never knew when – or if – you would see your sweetheart again.

For a special occasion like this I was handed small bags of dried fruit for the cake, sugar, margarine, even pieces of butter. My Auntie Joan made the cake, two tiers, wonderful. Liquid paraffin went in to eke out the fat. [Liquid paraffin was often used in wartime cake baking; in peacetime it was traditionally used to ease constipation.]

My wedding day started badly. I had a very bad cold. After putting my dress on and fixing my veil, blood began to pour from my nose down the front of the dress.

It was awful. No time to take everything off, so I lay on the bed and a board was placed between the dress and me and my mother proceeded to scrub the stain and then try to iron it – with me still inside!

The doctor was called, and he injected me with something to stop the bleeding.

Eventually I turned up at the church very late with cotton wool up both nostrils and a wet cloth in an oiled silk bag in my hand. I had no make-up on. I must have looked terrible.

The sirens were sounding 'Alarm' when we went into the church and sounded the 'All-Clear' when we came out. The reception was held in the Co-op upstairs in Alum Rock Road. Everything had to be transported by pram. But we had a good time as people had been very generous with their gifts of food.

If they couldn't afford a wedding present they gave you something of their own. One was a dish with some jelly still in it. We had two breadboards, three cruet sets – and some money!

One of my final clearing-up jobs was to empty the vase my flowers had been in. The lady who had lent us the vase wanted the vase back.

There was nowhere to throw the water so I stood on a chair and emptied it out of the upstairs window of the Co-op.

Unluckily for me a man had been passing underneath. He was very drunk and came marching up the stairs into the reception room wearing a wet bowler hat, water streaming down his face.

It was hard not to laugh. He was very angry, demanding his rights in a very loud voice. To calm him down, my cousin Len gave him two bottles of stout. He went away happy.

And so did Alan and I, for fifty-seven years until Alan died. I can honestly say I never wanted anyone else.

## 'WE GOT MARRIED TWICE IN THE SAME DAY'

Londoner Eileen Hunt thought she had her wedding plans in place for her marriage to her sweetheart Victor. Then the war changed her plans dramatically.

On Friday 10 May 1940, I was working in King's Cross at a furriers, making double fur coats for the Red Cross that were being shipped to Russia by the Merchant Navy to aid Russian children. The fur was musquash – very thick.

I was due to get married to my boyfriend Victor on Saturday 11 May.

That Friday when we finished work, someone gave me a bouquet of my favourite flowers, lily of the valley. Victor was in the RAF so I went to King's Cross station to meet him.

But the station was closed, swarming with police and soldiers. No one was allowed in or out. A policeman told me all leave had been cancelled. The Low Countries had been invaded by Germany. I wasn't going to get married.

Heartbroken, clutching my precious bouquet, I went home and cancelled the church, car and flowers.

Yet unknown to me, on hearing the news, my brother and brother-in-law had taken the initiative. They rushed up to Victor's base near Cambridge, kidnapped him and hid him on the floor of a borrowed van. They then drove him from Cambridgeshire to London under a blanket, all the way to Deacon Street in south London where he lived.

Because I had cancelled the wedding, I had to contact the priest. But there was good news. He said if we could get to the church by 6pm on the 11th, as we'd arranged, he could still marry us.

We managed it. I got dressed up and Victor appeared at the church – and the priest married us. But after the ceremony he told us the marriage wasn't legal as we had not had a registrar to witness the wedding!

Luckily, one of the congregation nipped out of the church and managed to find the registrar. Then we had a second marriage in the Lady's Chapel; the priest had us repeat our vows again before the registrar.

We had the reception in my sister's house. Then Victor was bundled back to Cambridge and sneaked into his camp. At his camp there was another airman called Hunt so Victor signed in as him. His friends had put pillows in his bed so it was not noticed he was missing. He was very lucky. He could have been up on a charge. But it was a month before we saw each other again.

We were very fortunate to marry that day. Several weddings were cancelled, and I think we were the only ones to manage it. One couple were stopped as they were about to enter the church. Victor and I were married for forty-nine years and had four children.

I always say Hitler didn't stop our wedding!

# CHAPTER 5

# THE RETURN

*'Your finest clothes are those you wear as soldiers'*
VIRGINIA WOOLF

The greatest aspect of the aftermath of World War II was the homecoming of the armed forces.

Because the war in the Pacific had continued in those three eventful months after VE Day, the authorities had believed that any attempt to demobilise Britain's Armed Forces would entail a protracted period of time – possibly as much as two years – in order to bring the troops back home.

Yet events took a different turn. The unexpectedly sudden ending of the war with Japan in mid-August meant that the process of servicemen and women returning to civilian life evolved into a shorter time than had been envisaged.

Some men and women were released even before VJ Day. On 18 June 1945, which had been scheduled as the beginning of the demob or return process (one month before, soldiers had been informed of this), a third had been demobbed by the end of 1945 – out of a total of just over 4.3 million men and women in the Forces and war industries. The remaining troops were eventually demobilised by January 1947 when millions of men and women finally returned to civvy street.

The greatest numbers of returnees, of course, were the armed forces. Most had been in the Army, Navy or Air Force since 1941. Nine out of ten were men, the majority wartime conscripts or volunteers. Some had previously signed up for service life and continued to remain in service beyond the war's ending.

Furthermore, millions of troops were abroad, a vast number scattered round the globe from Norway to Africa and to the edges of Antarctica: 250,000 of these had been overseas all the time for more than five years.

Some early Forces returnees like the RAF's Stan Ratcliff (in Chapter 2) would return to England in the summer of 1945, and technically remain 'in service', only moving into dispersal or demobilisation units that autumn.

The war's ending also meant a return home for many civilians, including the evacuated children heading back to urban lives as well as the adults returning home from an unfamiliar wartime job on the home front.

There were also returning prisoners of war. After Japan had surrendered, the shockingly barbaric treatment of the 140,000 Allied military personnel captured by the Japanese armies in 1941 and 1942 – at least 50,000 of whom were British – was revealed to the nation in cinemas' accompanying newsreel footage, the same type of documentary footage revealed in 1945 following the Allied troops entry into the Nazi concentration camps. Horrific and disturbing – yet the visual evidence told the world part of the story of the brutality of war.

Close to 200,000 British Forces troops had been captured by the Germans and Italians and had also spent many years in POW camps. Their overall treatment was not as harsh as that experienced by POWs in Japan and Russia, but many, especially those who had been sent to work in freezing or tough conditions in labour camps, returned home with their health damaged by their experiences in captivity.

War had dislocated so many in so many different ways; families broken up in their millions; men, women and children scattered across Britain and the world; damaged or crippled men returning to a country struggling to get on its feet.

The word peace heralded a return to normality. But could anything be 'normal' after six years of chaos, uncertainty, grief and upheaval?

## WE'LL MEET AGAIN

The return of the troops put a strain on marriages. So much had happened to the women who remained at home. As well as carrying out voluntary work and running the home in difficult circumstances, through rationing, air raids etc., millions of women and girls took paid jobs in munitions factories, contributing to the war effort, working long hours – and earning financial independence for the first time. A returned spouse might easily be dismayed or unhappy to realise that his breadwinner status had vanished if his wife had acquired financial as well as emotional independence.

The possibilities for post-war domestic tension were many. Men frequently found it difficult to return to a more mundane domestic situation after years of adrenaline-led combat and camaraderie.

Couples realised too that they had grown apart through their own very different experiences during the war. Infidelity was a huge tension. Meeting new strangers from other countries was not something the average woman in Britain had been used to – foreign travel was still mostly the province of the wealthy – but the war changed that dramatically. A hitherto faithful young wife might go to a dance hall only to be swept off her feet by a glamorous, free-spending, jitterbugging GI. For some, especially younger women, here was sudden romance – an experience they'd only ever seen in the movies. In fairness, Forces men, far from home, could also find themselves caught up in unexpectedly torrid liaisons. This was nothing new: by its very nature, the ferocity of wartime had a habit of creating extremes of behaviour that barely existed in peacetime.

Far worse, however, were the consequences of sudden wartime infidelity, i.e. illegitimacy, very much a 'secret shame' in the decades before and several years after World

War II. Abortion was illegal, with many women putting their lives on the line to attempt to destroy an unborn child. Or choosing, in utter desperation, to abandon a new baby. When the emergency water tanks around London for the fire services were emptied at the war's end, they revealed tiny corpses of babies, perhaps drowned or already dead.

It is not possible to estimate how many women found themselves in such desperate situations as a result of a brief wartime fling. Only the statistics of wartime divorce give an indication of marital rupture: divorce figures went from 12,314 in 1944 to 60,190 by 1947.

'By now I'm wondering if you are caring to get any letter from me,' wrote Kathleen Patmore in a heart-rending letter to her husband, Cyril, in the summer of 1945.

Cyril had been abroad on active service for three years. Now Kathleen was expecting a baby fathered by an Italian POW. 'I feel I must keep on writing until I see you again or you tell me not to,' she wrote.

The letter, discovered by the Metropolitan Police afterwards, was not clear whether Kathleen knew that her husband had been granted compassionate leave to return from India to their home in north-west London. What she was hoping for, however, was an intense desire for reconciliation for the couple and their four children. 'I know that you loved me, otherwise you wouldn't have been so hurt.'

On 4 August 1945, Private Cyril Patmore of the Royal Scots Fusiliers stabbed his pregnant wife to death at their home.

One month later, he was committed to five years' penal servitude on a manslaughter charge.

A week before, a similar scenario involving another soldier who had stabbed his unfaithful wife to death also received a conviction of manslaughter, rather than the mandatory death sentence for murder.

Tragic as these cases were, the judgements were not harsh; society, it appeared, had painfully absorbed the shock of how the experiences of war could wreck family life: the disruptions of upheaval, grief and infidelity were far from being unusual.

## 'FROM UNIFORMS TO CIVVY STREET'

Essentially, returning home for millions in combat meant a long sea journey, a reunion with loved ones and the handing in of uniform to don civilian clothes.

Fred Roberts (1920-2017) joined the RAF in 1938 at the age of eighteen. He trained as an armourer and became part of the ground team arming Spitfires in the Battle of Britain in 1941.

In 1942, on leave, he married his sweetheart, Mary. Weeks later he was posted overseas to India, an NCO in charge of a team of armourers. He was with the RAF at Allahabad, India, when war ended. In Bombay, he finally boarded the ship back to England.

The ship was the *Capetown Castle* of the Union-Castle Line. On boarding, some of the corporals and airmen were given duties that entailed controlling the queues on the stairways to the dining hall at mealtimes. Fred recalls:

I will always remember my first meal on board. It was teatime and we were given kippers, as many as we wanted, and as much fresh white bread and English butter as we could eat. The bread was baked on the ship.

I don't think we had ever enjoyed a meal more than that one.

It was a straight sailing to England. No zigzag and no escort. We returned via the Suez Canal, stopping at Port Said to pick up passengers. We were passing Malta late one evening. The island was pointed out to us by a tannoy announcement and we could see lights on the island. On this same evening we were told by tannoy that the Americans had dropped the first atom bomb on Hiroshima in Japan.

We arrived at the Firth of Clyde on 14 August 1945, but the ship didn't dock until the next day when we disembarked and travelled to Morecambe, where we were boarded at various guest houses throughout the town.

That day, my first day back in England, was VJ Day, the day the war in Japan ended and this meant big celebrations everywhere. As we had just arrived back from the Far East, everyone – and there were thousands of holidaymakers in Morecambe at this time – wanted to buy us drinks. There was dancing on the promenade, congas on the pier, free entry to the theatres for us if we could get away from all the hospitality offered and towards midnight a tremendous bonfire on the beach. I don't know where all the combustibles came from but I remember well a lot of seats from the promenade burning well.

I was to get three weeks' leave, one for each year of overseas service. We were highly entertained each night in Morecambe by both the holidaymakers and the locals, but the few days at Morecambe soon passed and it was a train journey to Stratford-upon-Avon, changing trains at Birmingham and a taxi ride to Mary's home village of Temple Grafton.

Mary and I had so much to catch up on this leave. We made a few visits to Stratford, empty now of RAF personnel, all the hotels returning to pre-war activities. We also did a lot of walking on our own and lots of talking and planning. Then there was another farewell on Stratford railway station, just like the one three years before.

In December 1945 I handed in all my kit and was issued with a civilian hat, raincoat, suit, shirts, socks and shoes. My discharge book was completed.

I signed for an advance of wages and a rail warrant to Stratford-upon-Avon. I was granted three months' paid leave and finally discharged from the service on 6 March 1946.

Advice for women on how to cope with a returned serviceman after several years' absence was plentiful in many magazines and newspapers of 1946. Articles like 'When your man comes home' offered sensible ideas. Here's what the *Daily Mirror* advised returning troops in October 1946.

- Be glad to be back. Say so as often as you can. You cannot overdo this, however much you repeat yourself.
- Be prepared for civilian restrictions. Many of you will have little idea of what has been going on in English homes. Don't expect too liberal a welcome in material things at least. If she produces a home-made cake or a roast dinner, ask her how on earth she managed to do it. Do the shopping for her one morning, too.
- Be appreciative. Tell her she's wonderful, that you're proud of her.
- Take over some family responsibility. For a long time she's been mother and father in the home, maybe part breadwinner too. Take over your fatherhood at once and help a little with the mothering too.
- Be prepared for changes in her. You should expect to find a more independent woman who has matured in war.
- Be affectionate. She'll be shy, same as you. Don't try to rush her off her feet or try to woo her too ardently at first. However much she's changed, she's darn glad to have you back.

The RAF's Stan Ratcliff described his journey back to England in Chapter 2. A few months later, in the autumn of 1945, he was at an RAF Dispersal Centre, waiting to receive his 'demob' clothes. His daughter Joan wrote:

He went round the camp 'clearing' from the different sections, including the MT (motor transport) section, the gym and the sergeants' mess, all the time wrestling with his thoughts and trying to decide if he was doing the right thing. Last on his list of places to visit was stores to exchange his uniform for civilian clothes.

Stan watched his uniform jackets disappearing over the counter and got a last glimpse of his flight sergeant badges on the sleeves. Was he really being a total twerp? He was already paid as a flight sergeant and would undoubtedly be made a substantive warrant officer in no time if he signed on.

It was the best rank in the Air Force – viewed with respect by the commissioned officers and looked up to by the non-commissioned.

'Are you sure about this, Flight?' said the stores corporal as he slung Stan's uniform along the counter and pointed in the direction of the rows of civilian clothes all hanging on rails behind him. 'Do you think any of this stuff will suit you?'

For a brief moment Stan hesitated – after all the war was over now and he would be entitled to a married quarter. Their housing problem would be resolved in a minute. However, he knew his wife Lily wanted him to come out – she had made that crystal clear and who could blame her after the past six years?

'Is anybody ever sure?' he replied. 'It's going to be a wrench, Corporal – there is no doubt about that – I was attached to that old uniform.'

The only trouble with the RAF just now was that it was a bit like the little girl in the nursery rhyme – 'When she was good, she was very, very good, but when she was bad she was horrid!'

The trick was to forget the horrid bits but it was just a bit too soon to be able to do that. A year later and he might have made a different decision altogether. It was a split-second decision that would affect the lives of the next generation just as surely as his ancestors' decisions affected his. All he could do was hope he had made the right choices.

He turned his back on his uniform and picked out a three-piece suit and a shirt and raincoat. He was even supplied with shoes and socks and underclothes, along with a trilby hat.

'I can't see me wearing that!' he laughed. 'It makes me look like a spiv. I'll give it to my dad and he can wear it down the garden.'

Stan was a standard size and so very few alterations were needed, but it would still take some getting used to. He had spent every waking moment of the past six years in uniform.

He got himself dressed and surveyed himself in front of the mirror, screwing up his nose at what he saw. He was so used to Air Force blue that he felt as though he was looking at someone else for a minute.

'I feel as though I am done up for a bloomin' wedding!' he laughed.

He picked up the rest of the civilian clothes that had been issued to him and stuffed them in his kitbag.

'Cheerio, Corporal, and good luck to you,' he said.

'Goodbye, Mr Ratcliff,' smiled the young NCO.

Stan flinched like he had been hit – that brought it home!

He smiled as he went out of the door meeting a queue of others who were on their way in for the same purpose.

There was no getting away from it. He did feel odd now that demob had finally arrived. It seemed like a life-time ago when he had joined and yet, in other ways, it had gone so quickly...

When he joined up just two days after his eighteenth birthday, he was sent to RAF Cardington. The Air Force then was barely as old as he was and it had been peacetime.

He had been part of the Guard of Honour sent to France in 1930 when the R101 airship so tragically crashed. It had been his job to escort the 'remains' back to England for burial and he had seen George V in person. What a memorable experience that had been for a young lad who never dreamed he would ever go abroad. He certainly could not have envisaged that he would be back there in a war nine years later!

He smiled to himself as he remembered the arrival of that brown envelope with OHMS written on it just before his wedding in 1939 as he strode out down past the billets to the sergeant's mess in order to say goodbye to some of the blokes. He was thirty-four now and couldn't believe where the time had gone.

When he was living through the years the time seemed interminable but now, looking back, the whole of his service life had gone by like lightning. Funny how the mind could play such tricks – and there had been such progress! He had been there when the RAF was in its infancy and he had been in the thick of it in the war.

Now, there was even talk of planes going 'faster than sound' – apparently as a result of the invention of the V-1s and V-2s. Things were moving fast.

However, most of the chaps who were being called up were fifteen years younger than him and many of the people of his own age had already left – or were dead!

He had missed out on too much already at home and he was not going to miss out on any more, despite his affection for the RAF. He couldn't spare any more of his nine lives.

He arrived at the sergeants' mess and said goodbye to some of the men who were still waiting to go into stores. Then he tagged along with a group of blokes, all of whom looked slightly uncomfortable in their civilian clothes, and they climbed aboard the RAF bus that was to take them to the train station. The bantering and laughter stopped as the vehicle went through the gates.

It was an emotional moment and all were lost in their thoughts.

## IS THIS DADDY?

For a small child, the return home of a father they only know as a khaki-clad man in a snapshot becomes a much-treasured memory of a joyful event. Little Ann Priest had just arrived at primary school in Hertfordshire when her father came home.

1945 was a memorable year for me. Peace was declared and my father came home for good – not just on leave – and I went to school for the first time.

Whitefriars School stood in a little town called Wealdstone, near to where the built-up areas thinned out to the countryside of Hertfordshire. It was a red-brick Victorian building with high windows and a tarmac playground surrounded by a barred fence. This was great fun to climb on or swing from at playtimes.

The infants – there were thirty-five of us – were in a large, high-raftered room. Green tiles around the walls reflected the changing light from the windows and at one end was an open fireplace where coals burned, warming the entire area. We soon settled in and became accustomed to the rituals of our new life except, that is, for the toilet arrangements. Until we left to go to the 'big' school, they remained the bane of our young lives. On top of the teacher's desk stood two packs of toilet paper, renewed each morning by Mr Hurst, the elderly caretaker. The ruling was this: the hand went up, permission to go to the "lavatory" was given and, under the eyes of thirty-four classmates, you collected the regulation two sheets and left the room.

Next came the dash across the windy playground to the wooden block of toilets, standing in solitary splendour in full view of most of the school. Four toilets under one roof, they were kept spotlessly clean by Mr Hurst and smelt only of damp wood and strong disinfectant. I have often wondered whether the knotholes were deliberately left in the wood to discourage long sittings. The draughts were incredible. The greatest hazard, however, was at playtime when those knots served as peepholes for the rest of the school. It was a hardened or desperate pupil who risked such embarrassment at these times.

I had been at school for about eight weeks when news came that my father was to be demobbed. I remember wondering what that word meant but decided that it couldn't be anything too bad because my mother was so happy. Gradually the atmosphere at home began to affect me. I couldn't wait to see him either. There was a picture of him on the sideboard dressed in khaki and I sat in the evenings looking at it, wondering what he would be like. He had, after all, been away for most of my life. Dad was due home on a Friday and Mother kept me off school.

All day I sat at the top of the stairs waiting for the doorbell to go. My mother was even more excited and kept going backwards and forwards to the front gate to see if he was coming. Eventually the bell rang, Mother opened the door and he stood there, looking up at me and smiling. Just like his photograph.

I threw myself down the stairs but missed my footing and landed at his feet with a thump. It turned out that I had dislocated my shoulder. My poor father, I don't know who was more upset. What a homecoming!

From Holland, he had brought me a little pair of clogs, brightly painted in red, blue and yellow with my name on the front. They fitted perfectly and, when my arm healed and I took them to school, I was the envy of my schoolfriends.

I have them still, next to that photograph of my father.

## THE POW'S RETURN

The history of Dunkirk, and the evacuation of 400,000 Allied troops from the beaches of France following the German invasion of Belgium, France and the Low Countries, turned a huge wartime defeat into a triumph in the summer of 26 May to 4 June 1940.

Yet for the 40,000 British and French troops in areas near Dunkirk who were left behind, the sudden defeat by the German army meant capture and imprisonment, even slave labour in mines, fields and factories in Germany and Poland.

Roy Pryor was one of these men. Roy was a RAMC field ambulance medical auxiliary (this was an unarmed non-combatant unit) captured by the Germans on 28 May 1940 alongside a group of ten men, all of whom were friends from Roy's hometown of Ashford, Kent.

Roy was just twenty. He had joined the Territorial Army two years before. His four-year imprisonment as a POW followed a miraculous hair's breadth escape – on the very day of his capture.

We faced crack German SS troops in black uniforms with a skull and crossbones. We'd had it. The men in black were shouting, yelling, screaming at us, herding everyone along the edge of a nearby ditch. Stunned by the speed of it all, we moved along. Two huge machine guns were being aimed directly at us. We were about to be annihilated.

A huge weight formed in the pit of my stomach. You could not break down. Fear of demonstrating any fear dominated our thoughts. If you were an unlucky one, so were many others.

But the guns did not fire. In a flash, everything changed. A German infantry group on bikes and gun carriers had been right behind the tanks led by the black-clad SS men. These SS guys didn't want to stop. They'd have gunned us down without thinking. But we were now in the hands of the ordinary German army; the SS cleared the way for them – and just swept through.

The German troops were shoving us, yelling, 'ENGLAND KAPUT' or other epithets. For us there was just overwhelming blanket relief: we were still alive.'

What Roy discovered after the war was that this same SS Panzer Division, known as the Totenkopf or Death's Head Division, had massacred a hundred surrendered men of the Royal Norfolk Regiment with machine-gun spray just the day before, a war crime for which their commander, Fritz Knöchlein, was executed in 1949.

Yet even as a relieved Roy and his friends joined the huge numbers of French and British captured men – on what was later described as the Dunkirk Death March – through France, they had no idea of what lay ahead.

Our march started, destination unknown. We were part of the chaos of the defeat of France. Then it started to pour with rain, captured in the clothes we stood up in. We marched all that day, soaked to the skin until we were led to a village hall where we were locked in. Somehow, we slept. Of course we were hungry by now. We tried to exist on hard tack biscuits thrown at us by the Germans. But next morning, when we resumed our march, we were already dispirited. The effect of marching twenty miles a day on long, straight, endless roads in the heat of a warm June day started to show. Thirsty, hungry, our only resource was each other.

At night we stopped and slept in the fields. Very soon our bodies started to react: exhausted, thirsty, hungry. By the end of the first week we arrived at Doullens prison. It stank. No sanitation. No water cart. The promised 'food' came via twenty packets of 'hard tack' thrown into where we stayed in a stifling room. By the following morning, on the road again, I was in a bad way. I was starting to get the runs. Dysentery.

Before we left we'd had warnings: never drink water by the road. By then, we were drinking anything; in a way, the thirst was worse than the lack of food. At one point we spotted mangel-wurzels by the road. Big mistake. Eat one and it hurt your throat. They are fodder crop. Cattle can eat them, they have strong stomachs. Not us.

Jack Staples, always a fit sort of bloke, spotted me, came over and without a word kept me going. Really, he was dragging me along. Through the day he dragged me, at one point hoisting me on his back. You just concentrated on staying alive. We had come through imminent death, and as survivors we got through because we were together.

What the Germans needed was labour. Women in Germany did not do war work like ours. Yet the Germans weren't prepared to cope with this huge number of prisoners. So those first months of being a prisoner were really the toughest.

At Cambrai we were squeezed fifty or sixty to a cattle truck, no sanitation, impossible to sleep. Then there was a longer journey, several days of which were ghastly. By now we were like zombies. Not one day at a time, more like one minute at a time.

Arriving at a railway station one of our group traded his wedding ring with a French prisoner who had a loaf of bread in his rucksack. Then another train and a trip across the border into Germany where we unloaded at Trier. Then … another cattle truck, equally horrific. The trucks would stop maybe once during the day but by now time seemed to black out. You just had to exist. Somehow. Until the destination, Lamsdorf. The POW camp had not yet been built. But this was luxury, you just lay down on straw. We got soup, at least.

The straw was not a gift. Soon we were covered in lice going into the seams of your clothing where they lay eggs. Picking the lice out of your crotch or seams of your clothes then killing them became a way of life.

I wound up in Lamsdorf for fifteen months. As non-combatants we were forbidden to work. Our families waited months before they learned we were OK. We were 'missing'. We were told we could write home, one letter a month. But there were no Red Cross parcels.

After Lamsdorf it was a camp in Teschen, on the border of Poland and Czechoslovakia, where I was separated from many of my friends. At the end of 1941, Red Cross parcels started to come in: tinned fish and meat, tea, soap (real soap!), fifty Player's (some men preferred the fags to the food). Everyone would pool the parcels.

Then we were told we were going back to Lamsdorf and would be repatriated!

Overjoyed. But the whole thing fell through.

By January 1942 the Germans decided they didn't believe we were non-combatant medical auxiliaries. Our pay book was not proof, they said. We were sent out to work. For a month I was in the tailor shop, repairing uniforms.

Then it was potato picking all day. Then in October/November 1942, the tough work: stone breaking with a hammer to break up stones to make roads. Heavy work in the depth of freezing winter: all too much for me, and my legs swelled up below the knee. By January 1943 I was in the camp hospital, then sent back for more stone breaking for a few weeks. Then I was really ill. The doctor said pleurisy; my lungs were infected.

I wound up in Posen in an isolation hospital, and I had exercises every day to get my lungs working. I didn't know it then but the Germans were aware of tuberculosis and how it could be spread. So then I was sent to Posen hospital, full of young wounded Germans from the Russian front. I had an X-ray there, then back to the isolation hospital. I was there for nearly a year.

In November 1943 I was moved to a camp in Kühndorf, where all my friends were. Now we were protected workers again. Thanks to the Red Cross parcels we were mostly well fed; by January 1944 the doctor said there was nothing wrong with me.

So by the spring of that year, we were paraded and told we were being repatriated. At last it had come!

We went to the station and waited. Then an ambulance train came in for us with every nationality you can think of: Indians, Palestinians, Aussies, New Zealanders, Americans, all of these chaps were 'de-used', definitely unfit. Good enough to send home. They were combat troops wounded in various places; a lot had been wounded in Italy and North Africa. The train took us to Poland to collect more troops, then, on the next train we were making for France. We went through Berlin which was an unbelievable sight, just a pile of ruins. Then through Germany and over the border to France. Eventually we were in Marseilles and on to the ship, MS *Gripsholm*, chartered by the US State Department as an exchange and repatriation ship.

Oh, there was so much exuberance on board that ship. We were so unbelievably grateful for the food, and being American it was excessive. You didn't get an orange, you got a carrier bag full.

Freedom and food!

Arriving back, England was like a fortress. Nothing was allowed in: it was one week before D-Day. That Sunday afternoon, 28 May 1944 when I arrived, it was almost four years since we were captured. Sleeping again in my own bed it was as if time had stood still; though by then, I'd learned to sleep anywhere...

---

Here is Roy's breakfast menu on the MS *Gripsholm*, 21 May 1944:

Butter, Bread, Swedish Health Bread, Pineapple Juice, Tomato Juice, Papaya Juice, Oranges, Grapefruit,

---

Apple Butter, Strawberry Jam, Grape Jam, Raspberry
Jam, Orange Marmalade, Honey, Oatmeal, Cream
of Farina, Shredded Wheat, Figs, Bran Flakes, Rice
Krispies, All Bran, Post Toasties, Puffed Wheat, Puffed
Rice. Bacon and Eggs, Boiled Eggs, Scrambled Eggs
with Pork Sausages, Roast Beef Hash, Boiled Potatoes,
followed by Coffee, Tea, Cocoa, Café Hag, Postum.

Dinner that same day:
Butter, Bread, Olives, Clear Mutton Broth, Roast
Leg of Lamb, Pickles, Wax Beans, Peas, Parsley
Potatoes, Peach Pie, Coffee and to order: Frankfurter
Salad, Preserved Pineapple, Apples, Pears, Bananas,
Oranges...

And he was still at war!

## MY FATHER'S LETTER

Prolonged separation from wife and children was one of the
more poignant aspects of returning from military service
after World War II. Philip Gunyon's father, Cecil, had spent
most of the war in many far-flung countries. He did not
finally return home until 1946.

Philip was born in Japan in 1932. In 1939, seven-year-
old Philip and his mother, sister and brother were en route
to Canada via Liverpool.

They were travelling on the passenger liner SS *Athenia* when the *Athenia* was the first British ship to be sunk by Germany on the day war broke out, 3 September 1939.

Torpedoed by submarine U-30 north-west of the coast of Ireland, ninety-eight passengers and nineteen crew lost their lives in the sinking of the SS *Athenia*. Philip and his family were amongst the lucky survivors. At the time Cecil Gunyon was working for an engineering firm in Brazil. Fortunately, Philip and family arrived safely in Canada in October 1939.

My mother, sister Barbara, brother Andrew and I arrived in Oakville, Ontario, in 1939. My father was a Londoner, born in 1899. After discharge from the British Army in 1919 he joined an English engineering firm in 1920 and was sent to Japan. My mother was born in Toronto and met Dad when he was returning home on leave in 1926. They married in 1930 and she moved to Japan with him.

My siblings and I were all born in Japan. We moved to England in 1938. Dad was then sent to Brazil in May 1939 and left us in England. When World War II seemed imminent he arranged for us to come to Oakville, near Toronto, where my maternal grandmother Maude Walker lived with her husband, Charles.

We lived in Oakville from October 1939 to March 1942, moving to St Lambert, Quebec, until September 1943. After that we returned to Oakville.

# THE RETURN

My father had returned from Brazil in 1942 and soon after he joined the Royal Canadian Navy as a Japanese interpreter. After being sent to Australia via Shanghai, he interrogated Japanese prisoners and finally returned home in 1946.

I was eleven when we lived in St Lambert, a happy time where I first learned to speak French. In winter, the roads were covered with packed snow and we all wore snow boots... Travel to and from school was enlivened by grabbing the back bumper of a car and sliding behind it in a crouched position. I can recall parades by khaki-clad soldiers marching down the main street and every family in the town with a plot of earth nearby would plant a 'Victory Garden' to ease shortages of fresh vegetables. During the war, everyone had a ration book, with coupons, just like they had in the UK. There were also special ration books for wine and spirits, used at the government-run liquor stores.

All through those years, Dad wrote to us regularly. He was away at the war all the time I was growing up. At first, the letters came from Brazil, then after joining the Navy they were postmarked Vancouver BC, Sydney Australia and Shanghai, China. They were eagerly read and shared by mother and us three children.

I still have a letter from Dad which he sent me for my twelfth birthday in April 1944.

This is what he wrote:

*My Dear Philip,*

*You and I have not been able to spend many birthdays together during the last few years, have we? I was at your birthday party in 1939 in England, but I left three days later for Brazil and I was out there when you celebrated your eighth and ninth anniversaries in 1940 and 1941.*

*I was with you in 1942 and 1943. But this year we will be 3,000 miles apart again when your birthday rolls around. Nevertheless, old chap, you may be very sure that I shall be thinking about you extra specially on the day and wishing you a very happy birthday and many happy returns.*

*The twelve years that have elapsed since you were born seem to have gone ever so quickly − and what a lot has happened during those years! For five twelfths of that time this terrible war has been going on − longer than the First Great War which we fondly imagined was 'the war to end war' and I just pray it will be all over before your next birthday.*

*You know, I was only six years older than you are now when I became a soldier in the last war. I just hope and pray you will not have to waste precious years of your life − at any time during your life − being a soldier or a sailor or an airman. I hope you will be able to devote your lifelong energies to making the world a better place for everybody to live in by peaceful and constructive means and not have to waste your time and energies taming the world's 'mad dogs' so many of my own generation have had to do. You young fellows have a big and terribly important job ahead of you and I know that you, Phil, will do your best to do a good job and that your 'best' will be a good 'best'.*

*I am very pleased with the way you have got along at school and the way you get along with people and your mother and I are both very proud of you. There are lots of men in this world who think they can get along best by adopting a blustering attitude and not caring about other people's feelings and by showing off, trying to act 'big'.*

*Thank goodness you show no signs of being like that!*

*Believe me, if you follow the Scouts' creed and be a gentleman you won't go far wrong. You can do no better than follow the Scout Law and the Ten Commandments. If everybody would do so this world would be a much happier place.*

*I seem to have been writing quite a sermon, which I really did not intend to do, but being away from each other so much I haven't the opportunities of talks with you which fathers and sons like to have together, and I just let my mind run on some of the things I would have been talking over with you if I had been at home. And I want you, Phil, to write me whenever you feel like it and if you have any worries. Don't ever feel afraid to write me about anything. I was a boy of your own age myself once and I know some of the difficulties and bewilderments that face a boy of your age.*

*And you, being in a class (in Oakville High School) with boys and girls who are all a bit older than you are, may run up against problems that other boys of your age have not yet run into. Well, if you do, please remember that I'm here to help you and don't hesitate to write and tell me whatever you feel like saying and you need not feel the least bit shy about writing me. That's one of the things fathers are for, you know!*

*Mummy tells me you found on a recent trip to Toronto the 'Stock Ticker' game you have been wanting.*

*[Stock Ticker was a Monopoly-style Canadian board game, introduced in 1937, where money was put down on six different stocks, i.e. commodities. Players then rolled the dice to see how each stock performed.]*

*Did you hear Jack Benny on Sunday night? He was broadcasting from Vancouver.*

*I listened to him over the radio at 4pm our time.*

*[Jack Benny (1894–1974) was a leading American entertainer and comedian with a huge following throughout World War II: his superb comic timing made him a legendary success.]*

*Well, old chap, once again, I wish you a very happy birthday and send you lots and lots of love,*

*Your affectionate father,*

*Cecil Gunyon.*

Soon after the war, when my father returned from Shanghai; a large wooden crate arrived from England where it had been in storage during the war years. My father opened it with his workshop tools. Inside were some of the treasures that had been left behind in our Northwood (Middlesex) house after our departure in August 1939. Amongst these was a brass coffee table my parents had bought in Japan, a small wooden statuette of a Korean lady and several framed prints and a hanging wall scroll from those same years. My sister and I still have these today.

Back with us, Dad settled into a new job with the Vipond Automatic Sprinkler Company as a fire protection engineer, much as he had been doing in Japan. That lasted until his death twenty-four years later in March 1970 when he was seventy.

I learned good values and always respected my parents – and the difficult times they went through to give us a good upbringing and education.

## THE NAVY WIFE

For some Forces wives, upheaval and long-term family separation did not alter in any way even though the war had ended...

Marjorie Batchelor (1908–2004) was a Navy wife. She married her husband, Herbert, in 1934. Bert, as he was known, had been in the Navy for some time when World War II broke out.

Throughout the war, the couple would only meet briefly for over six years.

In 1940, Marjorie moved from Portsmouth to Brighton to live with her parents.

I was sorry to leave Portsmouth but my husband wrote and begged me to go. He was very anxious that the war was not going to be short and that the naval towns like Portsmouth would come under attack soon, so I made all the arrangements. The furniture had to be left in Portsmouth: furniture removers could only move it for eight miles, due to petrol rationing.

The night before I left there was an alert. After that there were many firebombs which devastated the city. A few years later I made a return visit and the town centre was almost unrecognisable.

Brighton, then, was comparatively quiet. Air raids had not started but there was a certain amount of tension and preparations were made. Volunteers were recruited for fire-watching and the Home Guard was formed.

In November came Bert's last leave while his ship was being refitted. Air raids had started by then and he got detained at Portsmouth train station with three others.

They had to dive under a table in the waiting room. When the all-clear went, he rushed for the Brighton train and left his cap behind.

He arrived home at 2am, and I'd waited up. I was very relieved to hear the knock on the door.

He had his gas mask and tin helmet but the next day he realised he wouldn't be able to go out without his cap as civvy clothes were not allowed. I went to various gents' outfitters (to buy a cap) but if they had the right cap they didn't have the right badge for it.

In desperation, I looked at the King Alfred swimming baths on the seafront which had been commandeered by the Admiralty. Feeling rather daunted, I approached the two armed sailors at the entrance and tried to explain my husband's predicament. They listened impassively but when I produced his identity cards, I was taken inside to the petty officers' stores and, after some questioning, came out triumphantly with the required cap and badge.

This took some time. When I got home Bert said, 'Knowing you, I thought you might have got a train to Portsmouth if you couldn't get the cap here!'

Two months later, I realised I was pregnant. I told my family.

My father was less than enthusiastic. 'Bloody fools,' he said. 'Fancy after seven years starting a family when there's a war on!'

My daughter Valerie was born on 31 July 1941. Friends and neighbours were very interested as, after seven years of childless marriage, they'd given up on me.

At the end of 1941, the Japanese bombed Pearl Harbor. It happened so suddenly, overnight, it was unbelievable. So in 1942 the Americans entered the war and sent ships, planes and troops to England. While doing their training here, they made their presence felt, much to the resentment of some of our soldiers. They attracted the women and girls with their gifts of nylons, cigarettes and candy and were dubbed 'overpaid, oversexed and over here' by men whose wives and girlfriends were lured away from them.

We became acclimatised to the conditions and tried to live life as normally as possible. I'd make a visit once a week to my husband's parents in nearby Lancing.

Valerie was fourteen months old. We left their house soon after tea and as there were no street lights and the names of stations were blacked out, you had to keep count.

Once, we had just got to Shoreham when the dreadful siren started, the trains stopped, lights went out and we were sitting there for nearly an hour. Valerie went to sleep. Then the all-clear sounded thankfully and we reached Brighton station. Luckily it was still light and I hurried home with Valerie in her pushchair.

Back home, listening to the news, we heard: 'The Admiralty regrets...' There had been a heavy raid on a convoy returning from Russia. HMS *Somali* had broken in half and next of kin were being informed.

I sat at the table, numb with shock, for I knew my husband was on that ship. Two days later I received a telegram saying 'safe and well'. My relief knew no bounds.

By 1944 the Allies were on the attack and starting to liberate some of the occupied countries. The bombing of Britain still went on. Buzz bombs were dropped on London and the Home Counties followed by V-2 rockets, but not so much on the coast. In August my husband got a few days' leave and was able to come and join us. We all had a wonderful time together.

Two months later I realised I was pregnant again and decided to find a place of my own. Some weeks earlier I had heard from the furniture depository in Portsmouth that it had been bombed. My furniture had been moved to a church hall in the town. I was lucky. Many people had lost their belongings in this way.

I managed to find a Hove firm who were willing to bring furniture from Portsmouth to a lock-up garage.

I found a basement flat near the Seven Dials and after Christmas 1944 we moved in. It was not exactly a dream home, having once been the servants' quarters of a big house. It still had the jangling bells to summon the servants inside the front door.

The kitchen floor was stone and there was an outside toilet. In a narrow room opposite the kitchen (which I imagined was for storing meat because it was so cold) the landlord had put in a bath. It had a small gas boiler beside it, which had to be filled from the kitchen tap. However, we managed.

In spring 1945, my son Peter was born. In the meantime my husband was drafted to the *King George V* battleship which was on its way to Australia, and two weeks later he received a cable telling him of Peter's birth. The first supply ship reached them near Trincomalee, Ceylon [now Sri Lanka], with cases of bottled beer for the first time ever, so our son's entry into the world was well and truly toasted. It was nearly a year before Bert returned and I took Valerie to Portsmouth the day the ship came in.

We were allowed on board and provided with huge mugs of tea and we looked on in amazement at the large bowls of sugar on each table. My husband didn't seem to have many clothes but had a large kitbag filled with tinned fruit and one small banana. I wanted to eat the banana but I gave it to Valerie. She promptly spat it out. When, as a treat, I put some sugar and tinned cream with it, she spat it out again: so nobody had it.

It was 1946 and life as a family resumed again. Bert travelled to and from Portsmouth each day but then gradually he became unwell and was diagnosed with malaria. He was given sick leave and had to take lots of tablets which I'd keep in the wardrobe so the children couldn't reach them. After a month he reported to the naval doctor who said all he needed was sunshine.

One day, he didn't come home at all.

I was so worried that night. Next day I had a letter from Liverpool saying he would write again to explain. The next day I received his ration book which I had to hand in to my grocer, and by the second post came a parcel of his thickest clothes.

Another letter came saying he was on his way to Australia via Malta. I thought: 'Oh no, not again.'

It was to be an eighteen-month commission 'with light duties' and there was nothing we could do about it, except be thankful, especially if it was going to help him regain his health.

The man who lived next door came home and soon there were many more men walking around in their demob suits.

I'm afraid I felt rather envious when I saw them. And sad that my husband had to miss so much of our children's young lives and that they had not been able to get to know him more.

I tried to keep memories of him alive with photos and by reading out his letters. In the summer I'd take the children to picnic by the still empty paddling pool, hoping it would soon be filled again. Somehow we managed to give them little parties on their birthdays and swap rations. We exchanged tea coupons for sugar and made cakes with dried egg as we were still only allowed one egg each month. We conserved that ration, to be used for a treat on Sundays.

The eighteen months passed and Bert came home from Australia bringing with him a lovely doll for Valerie and a koala bear for Peter which was white with brown leather feet. Peter loved it. He talked to it non-stop, much to people's amusement.

My husband was then offered a job on the HMS *Sussex*, a gunnery training ship in the canal at Aldrington Basin in Portslade. This lasted for three years and as he was home each evening he decided to accept, to give himself time to acclimatise to civilian life.

My husband found it difficult to settle down in the basement flat. I looked forward to moving but had got used to it; in fact I had been glad to be there when the air raids were on. I never had to disturb the children, day or night as I felt we were as safe there as we would be anywhere.

In 1950, with the help of my father, we were able to put a deposit on our first home in Portslade. We thought it was wonderful. The children loved the long garden which had thirteen apple trees and there were schools for them nearby. There were horses in the paddock at the end of the road and some stables in the old village.

So began a new decade and a new life after the war for us all.

## THE CHILD EVACUEE

Alan Everett, from a working-class family in Dagenham, Essex, was just ten years old as war ended and he returned home after his evacuation to Somerset.

My arrival home was not one of great welcome and my sense of relief was ephemeral. Mum and Dad were involved in their quest to obtain the best living possible. Mum worked all through the war making gears for aircraft engines at Ford. She would leave home in the early hours and return after dark. She wore the regimental dress of all factory workers of the day, a turban with a knot at the front, and a cigarette dangling from her mouth. Yet she kissed me often and that alone brought great comfort – sharp contrast to the ambivalence shown before.

Our new home was another council house, in Hedgemans Road, also in Dagenham. We had graduated to a two-bedroom house. Hot water for a bath – then every Friday night – was heated in a copper coal-fired boiler downstairs and, when hot, pumped by hand to the bath upstairs.

Our bath salts to make the water soft were a handful of soda crystals. My mother would then dry me and my brother with all the vigour she could muster, our skin then as red as a turkey's crop. They say that Victorian men were much stronger – and it is easy to understand that the days of sail took no prisoners, but must have added to their virility.

For us, austerity was commonplace. For breakfast my mother would cut bread into small cubes, pour hot water on them and add a dash of milk. Our refrigerator was a bucket of cold water placed in the porch in which we would immerse pints of milk.

My father would hardly make time for my younger brother, or me, and very rarely showed us affection. What could we expect from someone who had himself had such a harsh upbringing? Being orphaned at fourteen does not give one a good insight for the future. However, we loved him dearly; if you have never received love you cannot show it.

During his early years of marriage to my mother he obtained a job on the London County Council as a decorator. Despite the fact that his knowledge as a decorator was nil, he had to get bread on the table and thus he masqueraded and survived. This was a very steady position and a regular although meagre wage, but this was all the work he could get and he was glad of it.

Nevertheless, he was still a man of inward importance. He had never forgiven my mother for putting "Painter's

Labourer" on my birth certificate. At the time, he said there were just no jobs available, and such was the suspicion of the working man he said that if a bus driver had a regular job he just would not speak to you, proof that the class system existed in all circles.

He once told me that in the deep Depression, he was standing in a crowd hoping to be selected for work. When the work processor shouted out work for one, such was the hunger of men with families that the crowd surged forward – and in the process a man was trampled to death.

When you're poor, you're poor. These were the days when if I was ill my mother would reluctantly call a doctor, because he would charge five shillings or seven and sixpence, depending what he thought the severity of the illness was. And that was cash up front before he had looked at you.

My arrival at Campbell Junior was one of anxiety, as I was allocated to the class of Miss Ryan, a spinster, with snow-white hair and horn-rimmed glasses, who would look over the top of them as teachers often do, and survey us like the Gadarene Swine.

I was by now an accomplished English writer in the mode or pattern which was given the name 'Barking Writing'. It was no problem for me but Miss Ryan thought otherwise, and even called the headmaster to endorse her view.

English being my strongest subject I realised that all my efforts counted for nothing here and I was promptly set hundreds of lines to improve on my apparent illiterate hand.

Miss Ryan was the middle-class teacher of the day, who always travelled Thomas Cook and ate Danish bacon; this was interesting to me because I had heard of neither of these names, and the only bacon I knew was a boy called Bacon. Nevertheless, I learnt that if you travelled Thomas Cook, their representative always met you at Waterloo station to direct you, a mine of information for kids in the ragged school, but how would we implement such information?

As with all schools we had a school bully. He was a big ginger-haired kid always engaged in some form of violence. He lived on a small housing estate some two miles from the school called Scrattons Farm; the name alone struck terror into our hearts.

Scrattons Farm Estate backed on to the marshes that run down to the River Thames, some two miles walk. Stretched across the river were two huge pylons carrying electricity to the south side. Evidently the ginger-haired bully had climbed these pylons for a dare, and in the process had touched a live cable at the top and fell to his death. I can recall the horror when I was told at school assembly.

My time at the junior school was brief, and at the age of ten I found my move to Campbell Senior School was a natural progression. I cannot recall having ever sat the eleven-plus exam. Nevertheless, I did at a later date pass the entrance exam for Clark's College School in Ilford, but because the quarterly fee was fourteen pounds a term, my father refused to pay.

My days at Campbell Senior were to be my career springboard. Our careers were not meant to go beyond the assembly line at Ford, and several visits to the factory ensued, the men standing in front of the furnace, wielding pokers some twenty feet long, and molten steel running in channels in the ground. I decided I would not be venturing in that direction, if I could possibly help it.

Teachers were violent in their approach to us. We had an astronomy class teacher called Mr Clay. He came from an approved school, and such was the violence meted out to us we had no reason to doubt him. He assured us he had taken guns away from boys, and who were we to disagree? By chance, we had one astronomy lesson in an art class. On the side a papier-mâché head was on a table. Mr Clay saw fit to pick up the papier-mâché head and smash it over a boy's head. It all dripped down the boy's face, without a word of objection. This was Dotheboys Hall all over again. Mr Clay terrorised most of the boys, and despite our toughness we trod carefully.

My arrival in the senior school coincided with a new headmaster, Mr Jones, a Welshman.

Mr Jones was a tall man, six foot three inches, dark hair pushed back with a parting, good-looking. He sported a military moustache which almost hid his thin lips and cruel mouth. When he addressed us his top lip curled downwards, and we knew immediately we were the dregs of the earth in his eyes.

You could easily be taken in by him, he was charming. On the surface. However, for our strata of society, he was the man for the job.

Cruelty made him tick. two days into the job one boy received a punishment so great the blue weals on his fingers stood above the finger itself, as thick as the cane he had used, and such was his injury his mother visited the school. (This was unusual in those days, as most parents assured us we must have deserved any misfortune.)

Evidently the boy's mother asked him at the interview, 'Does your conscience prick you?'

'Not at all,' he replied. 'This boy is unruly.'

Having seen she was going nowhere with this vicious animal, the mother resigned herself to the inevitable and dropped the matter. What authority would listen to her, an ordinary housewife to a boot repairer?

Little did we know that the headmaster Mr Jones gained adrenaline from this daily routine. He would always pick one boy at daily prayer assembly; you hoped it would not be your day. Like a drug addict he calmed down very quickly after his fix. I was a regular recipient of his wrath, and he could easily dream up some misdemeanour. In his onslaughts in his study one day I stood up for myself and questioned his action at the same time pulling away from his cane. He lashed out and caught me under the ear. To this day I cannot hear properly.

Nevertheless, we ran with the tide. He made sure the lavatories were clean and we washed afterwards, and woe betide the boy who left the basin dirty. Some years later in early adulthood I met him in a country pub. Much to my astonishment he introduced me to his friends as one of his old pupils.

Our senior days were not all unhappy. We would attend the outdoor swimming baths from March onwards and Mr Gant, our swimming teacher, showed us great kindness. He was instrumental in us gaining the bronze medallion for lifesaving and our swimming was a great outlet for the ongoing hatred of Mr Jones.

Weekends were very special. We'd cycle many miles and fish the beautiful lakes of Essex; wonderful happy years and friendships forged for life.

Whenever I go there today I always look to the rivers, which give me a great kick.

## CHAPTER 6

# LIFE AFTER 1945

*'Down in the jungle, living in a tent,*
*better than a prefab – no rent'*
COMEDIAN CHARLIE CHESTER, IN 1946
BBC RADIO SHOW *STAND EASY*

Wars, by tradition alone, cost a small fortune and World
War II had drained Britain of cash and many reserves of
gold, dollars and foreign currencies.

Rationing, controlling food and other prices, as well
as campaigns for National Savings and high taxation, all
mopped up surplus spending power in wartime.

The millions of personnel drafted into the armed forces
or the munitions factories had started to earn higher
wages during the war – at the very time when many
of the things people could spend their earnings on was
greatly reduced.

By the end of the war, perhaps unsurprisingly, there was huge potential demand for people to spend on clothes, household goods, cars and holidays. Yet as war ended, the country was facing a sudden economic crisis.

When the Japanese war ended, the US government ended their Lend-Lease policy. Enacted in March 1941 after the US had joined the war, the Lend-Lease programme supplied the UK and Commonwealth, France, China, the Soviet Union and other Allied nations with food, oil and material, including warships, planes and other weapons.

Technically this was aid for free – which suddenly vanished in 1946. Unless massive imports could replace Lend-Lease supplies, Britain would be desperately short of imports like food, oil and other essentials – which could only be had from America.

Britain then had to negotiate a massive loan from Washington to pay for Britain's imports. A Dollar Loan Agreement was signed with the US that year. The idea was to set the UK economy on its post-war feet immediately. Yet a year later came another crisis: the loan, after 1947's unexpected harsh winter and coal shortage, proved insufficient.

All of war-torn Europe needed US dollars and yet again the US provided them through Marshall Aid, giving European countries, including Britain, $12 billion worth of help.

From 1948 to 1950 Britain drew substantially from Marshall Aid, yet the following year after the outbreak of the Korean War, Britain was again pushed into the red: its imports were costing more, its exports dropped in value and its defence costs were doubled.

The post-war years were, in short, a very nasty economic tightrope for Britain. Such was the debt hangover down the years it emerged that Britain had still owed the US and Canada $83.25 million (equivalent to £42.5 million today) when its wartime debt to the US was finally repaid in December 2006.

Yet 'broke Britain' after the war had a somewhat positive side. While it had been generally assumed – mostly because of Britain's severe unemployment experience of the 1920s and 1930s – that post-war Britain would be facing serious unemployment, this did not eventuate, despite a blip in unemployment.

World War II was followed by a continuous period of full employment. The blip was the sudden 2 million unemployment caused by the freezing 1947 coal and snow financial crisis, but the level of unemployment recovered and over the next twenty years after the war the UK's unemployment rate averaged under 2 per cent.

As the country slowly started to get on its feet, there was a substantial increase in output in areas like manufacturing, engineering, metals, chemical and electronics. Millions of workers were employed in the heavy industries like coal mining, ship building, and iron and steel making. The fast-growing motor car industry – and the high demand for cars – meant that by 1950 Britain was producing half the total European output for them.

In a way, the story of Britain's post-war economy was a case of truly perilous swings and roundabouts. Yet at home, the looming shadow of day-to-day austerity dominated people's lives.

Food rationing continued and bread was rationed in 1946. The following year brought increased meat restrictions. Clothing remained rationed until 1949. Only in 1950 did petrol rationing end. All wartime rationing finally ceased in July 1954 – nine years after the end of the war.

Despite all this, there was some good news coming. For instance, the number of cars on the road rose from 2 million (at the outbreak of World War II) to 5 million during the six years after 1945. By 1956 car ownership had increased to one household in four.

Along with access through car ownership, seaside holidays became more popular than ever, with beaches finally cleared of mines. B & B landladies and hotel doors reopened wide – and families flocked in. Britain's seaside holidays had witnessed a Golden Age in the 1930s, so they very quickly started to draw holidaymakers in large numbers.

Holiday camps, where large numbers of families could be housed under one huge area complete with accommodation and all manner of entertainment and dining, also proved popular pre-war, with the most well-known camps like Butlin's in Skegness reopening in May 1946.

Newer holiday camps quickly opened. Pontins first-ever holiday camp opened in 1946 on the site of a former US Army base in Weston-super-Mare. Pontins subsequently opened six similar camps, smaller and less expensive than Butlin's. The all-inclusive affordable price drew millions of families into spending their break at these sites.

In cultural breakthroughs, Britain hosted the Olympic Games during the first two weeks in August 1948, the first Olympics for twelve years. These were also the first Olympics to be shown on television, which had recently been relaunched by the BBC in 1946.

In 1948 there were only a small number of TV sets in circulation. Yet an estimated 500,000 TV viewers, all living within fifty miles of London, watched the summer Olympic Games as the city, still bearing the very obvious physical scars of the Blitz, basked in a heatwave. (Only in 1953, prior to the Queen's coronation, did TV ownership start to soar when 2.5 million TV sets were purchased. This was the beginning of Britain's TV culture.)

The cash-strapped Attlee government had earmarked £750,000 to fund the Games. Yet it was viewed as a success – turning in a profit of £29,000.

Athletes were housed in former RAF camps and members of the British team subsidised their rations with protein-boosting whale meat. (Whale meat had been available unrationed during World War II but it was unpopular with households; the smell was unpleasant and the taste, at best, was bland. After the war, it was sold as 'whacon' by the Ministry of Food as 'corned whale meat with the fishy flavour removed', heavily promoted as high in nutrition. It still remained unpopular.)

These were very much the Austerity Games: many of the fifty-nine participating teams had to bring their own food. Bedding was laid on – but teams had to bring their own towels.

* * *

Given the large numbers of women who had been working during the war, many working in munitions factories all over the country, most quickly found jobs returning to work in the same factory site as munitions work ended and factories resumed peacetime production. Retail workers too discovered an increasing number of jobs for women.

Kathleen Wilson continued to work in the same Brighton grocery store she had worked in during the war. As a twenty-year-old, she quickly noticed how post-war lives were changing.

As time went on men and women were being demobbed. The return to their old jobs did not run smoothly. The women seemed to cope with it much better than the men … Women came out of the military service with changed ideas. No longer were they going to be slaves to the kitchen stove. They were much more independent now and openly desired a status of their own in the community.

Some of the men were content to rejoin the family life and all its responsibilities but the greater percentage of them found no joy in this. Life in Civvy Street was suddenly undesirable after the excitement of fighting for one's country. They had no wish to settle down in the office

working regular hours from nine to five. They were inde-
cisive and restless and wanted better things for themselves.

Because of this attitude, a lot of women who held
men's jobs during the war found that their jobs were still
secure. I was one such person. None of the men who did
my job in pre-war days wanted to return to it, and since
it appeared that I was very efficient, I was allowed to
continue in my position.

The boss, Molly Mitchell, was not so lucky. About
eighteen months after hostilities ceased, she dropped
her bombshell.

One Monday morning as we congregated behind the
counter she said out of the blue, "You had all better pull
up your socks and smarten up your ideas now. Next week
there will be a new manager here in my place."

In the silence that followed you could hear a pin drop.
We stared at her in utter dismay. What a way to start
a week. We had not expected such a thing to happen.
Molly Mitchell was strict and no one refuted it, but she
was also fair. She was also understanding and could take
a joke as well as give one. We all felt she was one of us.
The idea of losing her was appalling. We all felt we could
not tolerate a man in her place. The only good thing we
salvaged from the whole affair was that, for the moment,
she would still stay on as undermanager.

She knew the man who was coming, but beyond
telling us his name she said nothing else. During the
week that followed, we watched her moving out of the

flat above the shop as she moved all her belongings to her sister's house in Patcham. We felt it was the end of an era.

The following week we all assembled outside the shop with a strong feeling of trepidation – and natural curiosity. We all arrived five minutes earlier than usual. Molly Mitchell was very non-committal. We assumed the new manager, a Mr Cooper, had moved in over the weekend. Now at last the moment arrived when we would see him and the climax came as the shop door opened with a decisive swing.

Not one of us had the courage to openly stare at him. We all filed past silently, which was very unusual for us and went to our allotted places to change ready for work. Only Molly Mitchell paused for a few words of greeting to him before joining us. Then, five minutes before opening time, we took up our positions and Mr Cooper called attention to himself as he stood in the middle of the now illuminated shop.

He looked a little younger than we had imagined him to be. He was tall, very thin, with dark-rimmed glasses and slightly wavy dark hair. He would have been considered good-looking by us if he only relaxed his features into the semblance of a smile. He hoped we would all get on well together and work willingly as a team.

He expected from us efficiency, punctuality, obedience and prompt service for all the customers.

We got over our initial shock. We made allowances for him. It was well known that a new broom sweeps clean.

We trod very carefully. Then we decided he was accept-able as a manager. After a month our first opinions about him began to alter. He was showing signs of abnormal strictness. We felt as though he was still the sergeant in the army and that we were now his subordinates.

Every morning RPDs arrived from head office. These were Revised Price Directives. They were pinned to the wall for us to read and commit to memory.

It was not efficient enough for him. He soon found fault in the way they were thumbed through when someone wanted to check up on the revised price of the article they were selling to a customer.

In his opinion they should have learnt it by heart on the first day of seeing it.

So he had us all lined up in the centre of the shop before opening, grocery staff on one side, provisions staff on the other.

This was the beginning of the reign of terror. Mr Cooper strode up and down between the lines with his hands behind his back as though he were at an inqui-sition. Suddenly he would stop and point his finger at someone and bark out, "Price of Bisto, Miss?"

He was not satisfied with one answer. Just when he had passed you by, he would swing round and point to someone else, "Price of Lifebuoy soap, lad?"

Mr Cooper's attitude did not encourage loyalty or any deep feelings of respect.

He was obeyed because he was the manager. The apprentices had no choice, as they were bound by a two-year contract. Come what may, they had to stick it out.

Life under Mr Cooper had to be experienced to be believed. Employees of today would never have tolerated the conditions under which we worked but we never knew anything different. We had no union to fight our cause and we had no pay for overtime.

I think Mr Cooper's rushing around was the result of nervous energy. He may have been domineering and a stickler for detail. But if one worked on it, you could begin to understand the way his mind worked – and so keep out of trouble.

Society had changed by 1945, but after the war, a seaside holiday was often the first option for families during that first summer of freedom in 1946, the first summer holiday for seven years for those who could afford a proper getaway.

In Coventry, where factories closed in late July, the local paper depicted 'thousands of people walking aimlessly through the streets or standing in queues for buses to take them a few miles away'.

Frequently that first summer people tried in vain to organise a seaside break, only to discover that accommodation had all been booked, such was the longing for any kind of break. Pre-war, the Holidays with Pay Act (1938) had been set in place. This meant that most workers were fully entitled to a mandatory and paid one-week holiday.

While package holidays and short-haul aviation were decades away, the first post-war summer, on the Friday before the August Bank Holiday weekend, (then taken at the start of the month) revealed huge queues waiting for trains to get out of London.

At Paddington, so great were the numbers that a notice was hung up: 'All platform tickets suspended'. (Platform tickets in the UK were commonly used on main rail networks until the 1960s; nowadays they are mostly issued in heritage sites as souvenirs for train spotters.)

A six-year-old Michael Proom remembers his family summer holiday vividly.

Our family went to Bognor Regis. The town had received the honorary 'Regis' after George V convalesced there after an illness in the late 1920s. The story goes that in 1936, on his deathbed, he was told he should soon be well enough to return to Bognor to convalesce again. Apparently he uttered the now famous words: 'Bugger Bognor'.

We stayed in a guest house or B & B just down from the beach huts at the Aldwick end of the town. Starched white tablecloths – and being personally served food at breakfast. One did feel grand. The first time we went was the first time I had ever breathed the salty sea air. We rented a beach hut, brewed our own tea and mum brought bread and butter and made us all sandwiches.

We went to various cafes and tearooms in the town for other meals. At one establishment we waited over an hour for our order before it was served by a young girl, totally gormless. As an alternative we would sometimes buy cod and chips from the local chip shop and eat it sitting on a bench in the park that runs behind the Aldwick promenade. Fish and chips wrapped in newspaper were the only fast food on sale then. Fish was available – it had never been rationed.

If I had to choose one single aroma that encapsulates the essence of the British seaside, indeed of the whole British way of life then, it would have to be that of fish and chips smothered in salt and vinegar wrapped in old newspaper.

On the road back to our B & B there was an ice-cream stand selling the most exotic ice creams ever seen. Mint, orange, chocolate chip, banana and tutti-frutti flavours were on sale. You could have them in cones or wafers, where you could get a better grip and a larger mouthful, if you held it horizontally. How did the vendor get so many flavours on sale at a time of food rationing? We would never know.

The real fun at Bognor was Hotham Park. Opened in 1947, it had every family attraction you could wish for. The miniature railway chugging around the grounds in clouds of steam, the boating lake with its small launches with real petrol engines – only adults could drive them. The park also had a putting green. Hotham Park was a fun place to be. It is still open today.

## 'I WANT TO GO TO THE SEA'

In 1946, Stan Ratcliff was working as a lorry driver for a family firm of Gabriel Wade and English, a timber and creosoting business in the market town of Walton-on-Thames , on the bank of the River Thames, Surrey.

Stan had settled into his work, delivering timber to destinations all over the country on behalf of his employers. He drove for long hours in his efforts to feed his family and save for a holiday at the seaside. It was a holiday that seven long years ago he had promised Lily they would have. The holiday that should have been their honeymoon.

He did sometimes think about the RAF but those moments were fleeting. It seemed hard to believe that this time last year he was still in Egypt.

Halfway through the school holidays Stan came in from work waving a piece of what looked like white flimsy paper in the air.

'Look what I've got!' He stood in the doorway and held a five-pound note up high in triumph. 'Holiday money – we are going to the seaside'

Little Joan, just started at infants' school, had never seen a five-pound note before.

'Ooh, Stan, let me look!' cried her mother Lily as she tried to reach it from out of his hand. 'A real fiver!'

She got it off him and held the large note gingerly in both hands as if it would bite her.

'Have a good look,' said her husband. 'It might be a while before we see another one. We are off to the seaside so get your buckets and spades.'

He was due a week's paid holiday so arrangements had been made to go and stay with relatives in Margate. Edie and Wilfred had bought an old bed and breakfast on the Kent Coast called Wilmarede made up from the first three letters of theirs and their daughter Margaret's names.

'We're not being 'vackerated are we?' said little Joan, getting suspicious the minute she saw the suitcases reappearing. 'I don't want us to be 'vackerated!'

'No, we are not going to be evacuated!' laughed Stan. 'Look, I have a five-pound note and we are going to stay for a few days with your Aunt Edie.'

Joan was very impressed when she realised the note represented five whole one-pound notes. She knew what a one-pound note was and if Aunt Edie lived near the seaside, then that was all right.

It was very warm weather and really the first year that anybody could go to the coast again. Children of Joan's age had never been before in their lives; the only thing they knew about it was from picture books. Wilfred knew this and so his investment would eventually become very profitable; he was certainly the businessman of the family. Not that it would cost Lily and Stan anything. All they would have to do was to take their ration books and contribute towards the cost of the food.

Any misgivings Joan had disappeared when she realised that her father would be with them and when they boarded the packed train with hundreds of other families, every child was carrying a bucket and spade. It was a long journey which involved a change of trains in London but everybody had the comradeship which only comes from being together with people that have all been through a shocking experience and who were all going to the seaside together.

She did notice the bombed-out buildings on either side of the railway line and the piles of bricks everywhere with flowers and weeds growing up through them. It was an awesome sight.

Every so often she nodded off to sleep and once Lily had the job of escorting her daughter down the long corridor of the train to the toilet. Lily and Stan marvelled at how crowded it was. It was as if people could not get to the seaside fast enough to make sure it was still there. The previous year the beaches had been covered in barbed wire and in many cases landmines. Even now there were only certain seaside resorts you could go to and Margate was one of them.

Edie was there to greet them when they finally arrived at the house just a few streets away from the seafront. They learned that Wilfred had got himself a job at Dreamland (a huge amusement park and leisure centre, still in existence today) which had just opened up again that year. In his spare time he was helping Edie 'do up' the house.

The following day they went down to the beach and all the children were totally overawed. Most had never seen so many people, all trying to find a place to put a deckchair, and people milling about by the pier having their photos taken and buying ice-cream cornets and sticks of rock. Stan paid a man two pennies and came away with deckchairs for Lily and himself. Joan could sit on the sand and make sandcastles.

'I want to go to the sea!' cried Joan.

Looking around it was hard to imagine that little more than a year ago the beach would have been totally deserted. It was well known that one of the last of the V-2s had hit the Kent coast, killing about sixty people all in one go. Stan removed his trousers to reveal his bathing costume underneath. Lily declined her daughter's offer for a trip down to the water.

'Go on you two,' she smiled. 'I'll stay and keep our place.'

Not that she was concerned about getting anything pinched. In 1946 a place on the beach was far more important to people than wanting what anybody else had…

That summer of 1946 was a very special time for the Ratcliffs. On warm evenings at home the family could sit outside on deckchairs that Stan had made himself and watch the evening primroses that grew all around as they opened up to the moon. All day they had kept their flowers closed but then one by one they showed off as dusk began to fall.

If Joan was allowed to stay up long enough she also got to see the eerie sight of stars in a sky so clear and peaceful that occasionally you could see a shooting star whizz across and then disappear over the horizon. The only thing to disturb the peace might be an occasional owl or bat circling around.

There were no aircraft in the skies of any description and even the fact of sitting outside at night at all was special, particularly when you were five like Joan and your father knows a lot about the different stars and he had used his ration coupons to buy some sweets. It was still a novelty to be able to leave the lights on and have nobody reminding you that there was a blackout.

A little screwed-up bag of toffees, a deckchair all to yourself in the twilight and your daddy by your side can make the world a very special place indeed.

For the infants the war was becoming a distant memory already as they were introduced to each new thing they had never had before. As well as bananas, there was their first orange, sparklers on bonfire night and real toys – even comics.

However, adults and older children could hardly forget and they were reminded every day in the newspapers and wherever they went, especially Stan who daily saw the devastation over vast swathes of London and the big cities that he delivered his loads to.

Younger children rarely got to hear the news or see the papers. Parents and schoolteachers alike decided that what they didn't know wouldn't hurt them.

It wasn't easy to shield them completely though, as day after day there were more revelations and the grown-ups invariably spoke amongst themselves and were overheard by prying ears.

Even Stan, who had been in the thick of it since the beginning, began to feel as though he knew nothing! He found himself reading about battles that he had been involved in and yet never knew the true extent of the casualties or the significance of them at the time. There were always pictures at the cinema of the wrecking of the big cities, not just in England but in so many parts of Europe.

Sometimes when Stan had a particularly long journey for the haulage company, he stayed overnight in 'digs' (a B & B) in Manchester or Liverpool and then came back the following day. Sometimes he went to the pictures with one of the other drivers.

There he saw Pathé News and stared speechless at the panoramic views of Hiroshima and Nagasaki, simply wiped off the map. And the dreadful images of what went on in the German concentration camps. It was unbelievable and something that nobody could talk about.

The men just stared open-mouthed at what they saw until the original film that they went to see became of no consequence at all. Then there were the shocking pictures of Malta being bombed and yet it still seemed like a bad dream to him and hard to believe that he had been underneath it all, watching it. Even the hospital that he had finally been invalided to had received a direct hit soon after he had left it. Once again he wondered how many of his nine lives he had used while he was there.

That summer, there was another huge issue facing the country: housing. The practice of squatting – people taking over and occupying empty premises – went back for centuries, often through desperation for a home, sometimes as a political protest.

The extensive bombing in the cities had destroyed homes all over the country – a quarter of all homes in Britain were destroyed during the war. At the same time, the servicemen were returning and the population itself was growing with a post-war baby boom. Since no new housing had been built since the war started, the huge demand for housing was exceeding supply – and then some. Even finding somewhere to rent in the cities was a nightmare.

One result of all this was mass squatting, which started in August 1946.

Former military buildings were an obvious focus for the homeless: many parts of the countryside had wartime Army and Air Force camps now standing empty, and the government could find no reason for denying their use as emergency housing.

Many of these empty camps were handed over to squatters. Some were groups of ex- servicemen. By the autumn of 1946, official figures recorded nearly 40,000 people living in more than 1,000 ex-military camps in England and Wales, with another 4,000 people living in Scotland.

This was a respectable form of squatting. Most of the squatters were not politically motivated, or wanting to overthrow private property: as the popular newspapers of the time made it very clear, these were just decent people wanting a home.

Opinion surveys at the time revealed that people saw a clear distinction between the occupation of private property and the use of publicly owned buildings such as old Army huts.

Then the public mood changed. In September, 1,500 homeless people started to squat in luxury flats in Central London, flats that had been in official use during the war. Squats were established in posh areas: Marylebone, Pimlico and St John's Wood. Uproar followed this news.

The government then offered immunity from prosecution for any squatters leaving voluntarily – assuring efforts to secure temporary accommodation for them. Within weeks, many had left the London flats to be temporarily housed by authorities elsewhere in the city. Many of the squatter camps around the country were handed over to the occupants. Later on, some were incorporated into a wider housing system used as social housing in the 1950s.

The squatters did not solve the housing crisis – but they made a very powerful point.

Peter Southgate from Woodchurch, Kent, remembered his childhood experience of squatting.

For a year in 1946 and 1947, my parents and I were squatters, though at the age of four I was too young to know it. Fed up with living in rented rooms, my father moved us into an old Army camp in the Cambridgeshire countryside. The camp consisted of a mixture of about twenty corrugated iron Nissen huts and wooden huts with pitched roofs.

We had one to live in and one as a store for our surplus furniture, books and other possessions – my father never travelled light. Water and sanitation were basic and an iron stove was as good as it got for heating. But it was home and we were grateful for it at the time. It must have been hard work for my parents, but it was exciting for me as a young child.

The camp was a safe place to roam and play in, and the social mix was considerable, for the homelessness created by war knew no social boundaries and there were people around us from all backgrounds. In one of the neighbouring huts I remember seeing my first electric train set in operation, cherished by its owners from pre-war days.

Hardly anyone had a car at that time and we were a mile or two from the nearest village, so the sense of community was strong. It was certainly put to the test by the weather that winter.

This was one of the harshest in living memory, and a wooden hut was not the best place to spend it in. First of all we were buried in snow for a week while men with shovels worked their way up the lane from the nearest village. A great cheer went up as their lorry came into view and we were finally rescued. The snow eventually melted, but then there was a huge gale, which one night almost tore the roof off the hut.

The following year we moved into a normal house with a few more mod cons. No longer living in isolation, we were now in a village full of thatched cottages.

But that year stuck in my memory, and over the decades curiosity has taken me past the site of the hut many times. Each time I visited there was less to remind me of what squatting meant so long ago, until eventually it all vanished under an East Anglian field.

## THE BIG FREEZE OF 1947

As Peter Southgate describes, the winter of 1947 turned out to be Britain's most severe and protracted spell of bad weather of the entire twentieth century.

Bitter, freezing, shivering times for families already struggling within the cloak of austerity and rationing. The Big Freeze lasted from 21 January to 16 March when easterly winds drove a succession of snowstorms across the UK.

On 29 January, the country experienced the coldest day for more than fifty years. The temperature in London was -9°C. Hundreds of remote northern farms and villages were cut off by 20ft snowdrifts. A bitter twelve-hour blizzard off the south coast brought shipping to a complete standstill. In Essex the drifts were 14ft deep. In Surrey and Middlesex, millions of commuters stayed at home.

As if that wasn't bad enough, the lights went out all over the country. Power cuts meant electricity was off for long periods, gas in many cities was about a quarter of its normal pressure and the huge snowdrifts meant that transport virtually ground to a halt.

'SCOTLAND ISOLATED' and 'ENGLAND CUT IN HALF' were the stark newspaper headlines.

'Everybody in England was shivering,' recorded the writer Christopher Isherwood. 'Two or three of my friends said to me: "Believe us, this is worse than the war."'

Through February, the Big Freeze worsened. Coal fires, then, were the main source of heating homes. Yet the coal mines were inaccessible, pithead stockpiles were frozen solid and transportation was impossible once the coal was ready to leave the colliery.

Coal supplies were failing to reach power stations in London, the Midlands and the north-west. In February, the news that came through the airwaves was devastating: electricity supplies to those three areas would be suspended, and families would have to do without electricity daily, three hours from 9am, two hours from 2pm.

The entire country was paralysed.

In some places that February it snowed for twenty-six consecutive days, and at one point the temperature in Buckinghamshire was -21°C.

Children were off school for eight weeks. The armed forces were called in to clear roads and railways of snowdrifts which were up to 20ft deep in some places.

The snow did not disappear until May. Even then the big thaw had triggered widespread flooding in March when thirty-one counties were inundated with water.

Yet again, peacetime had left the country taking a terrible battering. Stinging tax rises and cuts in domestic consumption afterwards did little to restore the gloom that hung over everyday life. The estimated cost of the damage caused by the Big Freeze was around £5 billion in today's money. Yet the overall impression afterwards was that somehow people had taken the blows and, in the memorable words of Churchill, 'kept buggering on'. Britain could – and did – take it. True grit.

## 'DON'T LOSE IT, THERE'S NO MORE WHERE THAT CAME FROM'

For Stan and Lily Ratcliff, the winter of 1946–7 seemed to go on forever. There was snow at Christmas and it was still hanging about as late as Easter. It had developed rapidly into a crisis; on top of the stringent rationing the coal for the power stations could not be transported by road and rail. Even Stan could not drive his lorry.

> He tried not to have a hankering for the RAF but it wasn't easy at this time. Life was every difficult indeed.
>
> By February, the electricity was cut off completely and only switched on twice a day and all the roads were in darkness. It was like the blackout once again. Even the wireless was suspended. There was no BBC Third Programme – not that anybody listened to it that much anyway – and all radio ceased at 11pm.

There was no coke for the stove to heat their home – a converted railway carriage – and Stan spent much of his time collecting logs and chopping them up to get some warmth to go around the place. Lily's electric cooker was no good without power.

Little Joan thought it was ever so exciting! You could put pennies on the inside of the window and melt the frost so that you could peer out as if they were binoculars. You had to be careful not to put your face actually on the glass though, because then it temporarily stuck! There were icicles all around the roof, making it look like Santa's grotto. Once it started to get dark, you had to use candles for lighting and they were pushed into melted wax in a saucer.

Stan still had to get to work somehow and undertook the perilous journey every morning into London, picking up what bits of shopping he could on the way back.

There were times when Lily wondered how they were going to get through this awful winter.

Even Joan got the job of doing some of the shopping. Lily wrapped a half-crown up in a piece of paper (the coin was equivalent at the time to two shillings and sixpence) with a shopping list on it and pushed it inside her daughter's mitten.

'Now don't you go and lose it,' she said. 'There is no more where that has come from.'

What was a very adventurous time for the children was a nightmare for the adults. It was so cold that at Margate, where they had holidayed, some of the sea froze over.

## 'THANK GOODNESS FOR
## THE 'JERRY' UNDER THE BED'

Dave Dutton was born in the summer of 1947 in Atherton, Manchester. His mother, Mabel, was twenty-five and a factory worker. During the war she worked in a big munitions factory in nearby Risley. Dave was born out of wedlock, the result of a passionate wartime love affair between Mabel and Stanley Grant, a manager at the factory. (Mabel had refused to marry him.)

Growing up in a small two-up, two-down Victorian terraced house after the war, Dave's childhood was warm and loving with a close-knit family around him. Yet as he recalled, it was very, very cold.

It would seem very bizarre to a child these days to live the life we led then. In winter, our house was so cold there were those frost patterns that looked like leaves on the sash windows. They were very beautiful and somewhat mysterious – but that was cold comfort to us.

We had to make a fire every morning from scratch by putting up a shovel against the opening and covering it with newspaper until the updraught got the fire going.

When things went wrong, it was great fun watching Mam jumping up and down on a burning newspaper in the hearth to stamp out the flames.

Just over the fire in the living room was a clothes rack which was raised and lowered by a rope attached to a pulley. The room itself was about sixteen square feet with a sofa, an armchair, a round table with some fancy inlay, an old Victorian sideboard with mirrors, a wireless and a gramophone that had seen better days – and so had some of the performers whose records we played. We had stacks of old seventy-eight records. By the time I was three I was singing Teresa Brewer's hit 'Music, Music, Music' from behind the couch for the benefit of visitors and relatives.

The kitchen had a gas cooker, a boiler and a big white slopstone sink (a slopstone is a stone slab) with a cold water tap. At least our house was lit by electricity, unlike my gran's sister Betsy Alice's house which had gas mantles. Astonishing. (A gas mantle is a mesh-type device for generating bright white light when heated by a flame. Gas mantles formed part of street lighting until widespread electric lighting in the early 1900s.)

Mabel used to 'donkey-stone' the steps to the house (to make them white or creamy) as to have dirty steps was frowned upon by the neighbours. (A donkey stone is a scouring block, usually found in mill towns in the north of England, to highlight the edge of a doorstep.) There was great pride about then. For instance, people still wore their poshest clothes on Sundays.

Sometimes the outside lavatory froze up, despite our pathetic attempts to keep it usable by putting a paraffin lamp inside overnight to keep it warm. I was always very wary of the lamp after a similar one blew up in a play-mate's face and melted half of it away.

Thank goodness then for the 'jerry' (a chamber pot) under the bed which saved us from taking an icy trip down to the end of the yard but which had to be slopped out in the morning like something out of Strangeways (a big Manchester prison).

With no proper bath in the house we had to make do with the old tin bath which hung on a nail in the backyard. This was filled by water heated in the old gas boiler and the water sometimes had to be shared to save money. It wasn't very comfortable in there as it was more like a tin coffin than a bath and the bottom scratched your bum.

I remember Mam telling me she was once having a bath in front of the fire with a wooden clothes 'maiden' (a wooden frame used to dry clothes) shielding her to keep off the draught when the insurance man, Mr Hartshorn, walked in one night without knocking. He flew down the road when she started screaming the place down.

There was always a constant stream of people at our door then: Jean, the office girl who came for the weekly rent as the house then belonged to the nearby mill owners. The gas and electricity men who came to check the meters, though we had to feed the meter with coins and frequently the electricity ran out causing us to fumble around in the dark for sixpence to restore the light. The coalman, the window cleaner, the paraffin man, the mobile grocer, fishmonger and butcher, the milkman, the religious types.

The gypsy woman selling heather and offering to tell your fortune, then cursing you if you didn't buy. The Betterware man with his 'useful' household knick-knacks like egg separators, salt pourers and towel holders. The tramp trying to obtain money, usually under the pretext of asking for a glass of water. The knife and scissors sharpening man with a fascinating contraption, part of his bike with a grinder attached to it which worked by pedal power. The street singer, probably some poor war veteran who wailed his song in the street until you paid him to move on. The travelling tally man who sold clothes and shoes that Mam paid so much a week for until the cost had been met. (One of them, a nice, round, jolly man called Mr Dawson, kindly made me a pair of stilts when I was small and I learned to parade proudly up and down our street on them.)

All these people along with our many relatives, friends, playmates and neighbours came and went in a constant flow.

It's a wonder the door had any hinges left!

## A ROYAL WEDDING

If there was any news event that lightened the gloom midway through the freezing winter of 1947, it was when families turned on the radio on 10 July to hear the formal announcement of the engagement of HRH Princess Elizabeth, heir to the throne, to Lieutenant Philip Mountbatten. The marriage would take place that autumn.

At the time, the background to the royal love story had not been widely known.

Elizabeth was thirteen when she first met Philip, seventeen, at the Royal Naval College, Dartmouth, in 1939. It was love at first sight and the pair began writing to each other throughout the war.

They were secretly engaged in 1946 but the formal announcement was delayed until after Elizabeth's twenty-first birthday in April 1947.

The royal wedding, which took place on 20 November 1947, was televised, even though few had TV sets at the time; most would go on to see the newsreel reports of the historic wedding in cinemas.

That year had provided other dramatic changes, as promised by the Labour government. Now, for instance, public ownership of a chunk of the British economy was integral to the new government's post-war policy. So electricity, coal, transport, gas, and other industries like postal and telephone services were nationalised. These newly nationalised industries employed around 2 million workers, mostly in railways or the coal mines, a boost to post-war employment.

Further, Britain's empire – which had covered a quarter of all the people on earth at the end of the war – was now crumbling. In August 1947, Britain's rule in India ended after 200 years. Bloodshed and chaos on the Indian subcontinent followed, while other British colonies were heading towards independence: Palestine in the Middle East in 1948, Malaya in 1957, Ghana in 1957. By 1967, more than twenty former British territories were declared independent. The relationship with those former colonies with what is now known as the Commonwealth retained strong links. But Britain was no longer a major power.

It's not surprising that at the time of the bleakest of these post-war years, the glamour and excitement of a royal wedding and love story lifted hearts anew. Glamour was in very short supply in those years of austerity – only Hollywood movie stars and royals had the power to bring it to the masses.

## THE PREFAB

Back in 1944, Churchill had promised a housing programme of 500,000 brand new homes.

In the event, 156,623 of these new houses, using prefabricated materials, each with a similar two-bedroom layout and mainly occupied by young couples with children, were built during 1945 and 1949. By 1955 a total of 1.5 million homes of this type had been completed, rented from local authorities.

The new prefabs did go a small way to resolving the huge demand for new housing after the war. Yet the problem of constructing new homes of any description was intensified by the shortage of raw materials just after the war. There was a dearth of skilled workers to help construct the houses and a slow, tortured process of approval for housing schemes. Demand continued to exceed supply for several years.

The prefabs were sometimes scorned by architects and commentators, calling them 'tin towns'. They were constructed in post-war aircraft factories with empty production lines, all constructed to an agreed size. Many were built on the side of municipal parks and green belts, giving those who had been living in cramped, shared rooms in inner cities a feeling of space and living in the countryside.

The prefab had to have a minimum floor space of 635 sq. ft. and be a maximum of 7.5 ft. wide. All prefabs had to have a 'service unit', which was a prefabricated kitchen backing on to a bathroom. Water pipes, waste pipes and electrical distribution were all in the same place, making them easy to install.

The house retained a coal fire but also a back boiler to create a constant hot water supply. Bathrooms included a flushing toilet, a man-sized bath with running water and kitchens had built-in ovens, a refrigerator and a water heater. Many were decorated in magnolia with gloss green on all additional wood, including door trimmings and skirting boards.

Concrete and asbestos were used, which was quick and cheap to erect. Those fortunate enough to live in them were overjoyed at having a fitted bath, constant hot water and a built-in refrigerator. These 'mod cons' had been unknown for most. Each prefab had a garden too.

The aim was that the prefabs would last another ten to fifteen years. In reality, people who lived in them loved them: many prefab estates survived for decades. A handful were preserved for history in areas like Ipswich and Birmingham.

A few families like Doris Bee's had moved into a new prefab even before that freezing winter of 1947. Doris's prefab was situated in the Silver Jubilee Park, Townsend Lane area, near Kingsbury in North London.

My husband was demobbed in 1946. At the time we'd been staying with my parents. My sons were toddlers: Edward, three, and Robert, eighteen months. So this was our first home.

We moved in the summer of July 1946. It was all electric, two bedrooms front and back. The only thing was, curtain material was on coupons (rationed) so at first I could only buy enough for one window. I managed to buy some plain material so I embroidered little flowers here and there.

We grew vegetables in the garden and it had a shed – which was an old bomb shelter.

It was very cold in the winter, and the curtains in the dining room would be stuck with ice onto the metal below the window. The boys' nappies on the clothes line would be stiff with ice.

But we loved it there. We stayed there for fifteen years. We moved out because they were pulling them down and we moved to flats nearby.

Birmingham and Coventry, both heavily bombed during the war, were amongst the earlier local authorities looking to resolve the housing problem with prefab construction.

Jennifer Wright was born in Coventry in the summer of 1943. Coventry had witnessed a massive bombing raid in 1940, a devastating attack that left the city badly damaged and in a state of shock. Jennifer, like similar youngsters in post-war families, only knew her father from a photograph. Her father, John Woodford, a young soldier in the Royal Warwickshire Regiment, had been killed in the battle for Overloon, a bitter conflict at a time when the Allies were fighting to liberate Holland in October 1944.

I was too young to have any memory of him. He'd been a young driver at a laundry in Coventry where he'd met my mother Winifred, who also worked there, and they married soon after the war started. There were always two framed pictures of my dad on our mantelpiece, one of them holding me as a baby.

You're told what happened but at that age, it really doesn't affect you; had I been older, it might have been different.

For a few years after he'd died we lived with my mothers' parents in their house.

My mum went on the council waiting list and eventually she was allocated one of the newly built prefabs in Holloway Field, an area on the perimeter of Coventry.

The prefab was lovely. Two bedrooms, a bathroom and a good-sized kitchen with a table that you could fold down from the wall. Fridge, cooker, a copper for doing the washing and a small living room. Finally we had our own place, just me and my mother.

Next door to us was a little boy called Graham, who was a bit older than me.

We'd often play out together in the garden.

We'd left behind us a house with an outside toilet and a dog. So having an indoor toilet was a novelty for us but no dog – just a tortoise in the garden. When I started at primary school, my mother found a job there working as a dinner lady.

Everything changed for us when I was about ten because my mother remarried and we left England. We went to live in Calcutta, India, a huge adventure for me in 1953, and a completely different life. I didn't return to England for good until I was twenty.

Sometime before we went to India, my mother and I went to visit my father's grave in Holland a couple of times. We stayed with a lovely Dutch family. He's in a huge cemetery in a place called Venray, liberated by the Allies in 1944. I've still got a letter Mum kept from the war. It's from the Secretary of State for War, offering condolences – and returning my father's medals.

Liverpool constructed the largest prefab estate in Britain with 1,000 prefabs built in an estate called Belle Vue, located on each side of the Childwall Valley Road in the south-east of the city, new homes for families whose lives had been devastated by the Liverpool Blitz.

Most of these prefabs remained inhabited until the end of the 1960s, and a really strong community spirit developed on the estate.

Nellie Rigby had married her husband, Bob, an ex-RAF airman in 1946. Later that year they were given a prefab in Belle Vue.

I was so thrilled when we got the letter to say we had been awarded the prefab.

It was a roasting hot day when we went to see it. I couldn't believe it when I saw the fridge – we'd never known anything like it. It had wooden floors – a lot of people stained them brown – but in time we bought lino to be put down. My husband made a table for the kitchen; it was rickety – but it was our table.

In the summer we all used to sit outside at 12 o'clock at night with all the windows wide open; everybody on the estate would be sitting on the steps, all laughing and calling out to each other.

If anybody on the estate didn't have something and you had it, you shared it with them; that's the kind of people who lived there. When they wanted to pull them down in the sixties, a lot of people were crying; that's how much we loved the place.

## NEW TOWNS

The planning of new towns to develop housing outside urban areas was envisaged during the war, but it was not until the New Towns Act was passed in 1946 that the development of these towns was under way.

A total of twenty-seven new towns were built in the UK in areas outside London, in the Midlands, North East, North West, Wales and Scotland.

Stevenage in Hertfordshire was the first new town planned to alleviate London's housing shortages at the end of 1946, one of ten new towns developed in the years until 1950. (The next wave of new towns to alleviate housing shortfalls came from 1961 to 1964; further new towns were built in the years 1967 to 1970.)

In the late 1940s/early 1950s, inner-city families were actively encouraged by the authorities to move to new towns and while they were a significant development in post-war housing, they were not as popular as had been hoped; overall their planning was frequently criticised for creating soulless, depressing architecture, despite the fact that they were frequently cited by authorities as positive areas to raise families. Many had some further development in recent years: 2.6 million people now live in the UK's new towns.

Gladys Reid was in her forties when she first moved to Bracknell, Berkshire. Until then she had lived in Corsham, Wiltshire.

Bracknell, thirty-four miles to the west of central London, was originally a village. Designated as a new town in 1949, it has the advantage of being on a railway line. It immediately struck Gladys as an ideal place to move to with her family.

There were plenty of jobs – leave one and get another one straight away – but because we didn't come from London, we were housed in some cottages that had to be pulled down, so we had four moves in three years.

Then my husband got a job with the Bracknell Development Corporation so we qualified for a new town house.

We'd discovered Bracknell when we went to stay with a relative for a holiday, and we knew it was built for the population overspill of London. We had a good look round, liked what we saw – lots of factories, new houses, lots of opportunities, so we moved in – and never looked back.

# CHAPTER 7

# AFTERMATH

*'CHOOSE YOUR DOCTOR NOW!'*

NHS PROMOTION FROM 1948

How did those last years of the 1940s start to dismantle the years of war, austerity and much else?

By 1948 there were indications – perhaps not yet fully absorbed or even considered by all – that bold steps towards a more positive future for many people had started to evolve.

Some were low key, hinting at an opportunity to embrace an unknown future. Others would surely have surprised many at the time had they learned that these future steps could survive way beyond the twentieth century.

As shaky and miserable as the late 1940s seemed for many ordinary people – 'worse than the bleedin' war' was the muttered exchange repeated across the land in homes, pubs and street markets – these hints towards a brighter future came, in part, from governments.

The rest came – as it would elsewhere in the post-war world – from the entrepreneurial spirit of those starting from zero, aside from energy and determination – with the insight to look around elsewhere for inspiration.

There is an unmistakable link from 1948 directly to the present day in the UK. Moreover, it is a link which anyone living in Britain in the twenty-first century will immediately recognise.

Barbara Rivers was born in 1925 in Wealdstone near Harrow, one of nine children. She married in 1944 and her husband was in the armed forces. By 1948, Barbara was working in a London factory, as she had done since her teenage years. Her husband was then working in the civil service.

Barbara's resilience and determination, so typical of her generation, propelled her forward – at a time when women were at the mercy of a post-war world that rigidly remained very much a man's world.

After the war, oh it was a miserable time. I was working as a tailoress in a small factory in Battersea, London. There were seven of us women working there. The boss had a shop selling ladies' clothes and he would get quite big contracts, so I was making ladies' and men's clothes. The wages were £7 a week.

My husband and I were living St John's Hill, Clapham, in a very small rented flat over a pet shop.

We were saving up. I wanted to buy a house, but it was difficult to save, so you had to be very frugal. No coal, freezing winter. No central heating then!

As for my family, we were all very close. My dad Tom was a bricklayer, and it was a very loving home. With six sisters, there was always someone around me. At fourteen, I started work, making Army greatcoats in Harrow. I did that through the war.

The war hardened you in a way. One of my sisters didn't see her husband for three years; he was in Burma. My brother Leslie was in the Air Force in Canada. Four of his friends – I used to play with them as a kid – didn't come back.

My sister Grace was widowed; she was twenty-one. This is the tragedy of war. Her husband was serving here, in the Army, on searchlight duty. One day he suddenly collapsed in the pouring rain. It turned out he had a burst appendix and tuberculosis.

They did send him to the Isle of Wight to recuperate. Grace would go to see him every weekend, and later they sent him home, but six months later he died.

I'm afraid to say I hated the war, particularly when the boys we'd grown up with didn't come back. You don't forget.

I loved clothes and would make most of my own but sometimes, with a friend, I'd go to Petticoat Lane in the East End to buy clothes, as there was a lady there we knew who was quite cheap.

She would never take my coupons, she'd just take some money off us.

One day we went there to buy and for some reason as we were walking down the road afterwards we suddenly realised we'd left our books with the clothing coupons behind. Disaster.

Yet the woman from the stall managed to catch us, to give us back our books. Oh, we were so relieved.

At work, the seven of us always got on well; probably because we were all in the same boat, all struggling, though most of the other women had children too.

You felt that if you had a job, you were lucky – and you looked after that job too, as you were very glad to have what you could get. The government? Well they told you one thing, and did another.

One girl I worked with, her husband was so mean she had to write a list of every penny she spent; it was terrible. After he went into the Army she got involved with an American. In the end, she moved out of where they lived and left him a note after she'd stripped the house bare. She left him a teapot, a packet of tea and a cup and saucer. 'I can't leave the milk because it will go sour,' the note said.

As for the power cuts, you could expect them at least once a fortnight. They could last for three or four days and then, of course, you couldn't go to work. So you lost money. You could go to the Labour Exchange and sign on; it was a way of scraping through.

By then my family were all married, gone different ways: one in Hillingdon, one in Stanmore, one in Carpenders Park, all spread out but we would always meet up.

At work we used to talk about everything under the sun. You could get away from Britain, emigrate, go to Australia for ten pounds.

Why didn't we go? We'd talk about it sometimes. The issue for us was always: What will it be like?' No one could afford to go without the £10 assisted passage.

Sometimes we'd decide it was a toss-up. Stay put or go to a new place. But the new place was somewhere you didn't know at all. With us at work we decided it was better to stick with the country you knew.

The thing was, if you're working but you're still poor, as we were, you tend to feel put down by life, so you don't feel you can jump up to say or do whatever you want. You follow the rules because it's safer. You needed to be very adventurous then to take a chance like that. After all, you did have a job and a place to live, you were scraping by … go away and you won't know the situation at all, it was all unknown.

I didn't go dancing much in the war but the Hammersmith Palais was one I went to afterwards. I would go dancing with a couple of girls I worked with. We always made a pact beforehand: we went together, we would leave together. I went for the dancing. You could dance all evening if you wanted.

After the war, it was really difficult to find somewhere to live. My husband didn't find the place, I managed to find the flat in London. A friend who used to work with me told me she was leaving the flat so I asked her to speak to the landlord.

He didn't even ask me for a deposit – most of them would want money up front – but you could come across a nice honest person in that situation, as hard as things were. I was very lucky in getting that flat. £2 a week. I would drop the money off into the landlord's shop which was below the flat. All very convenient.

I'm a saver. But unfortunately my husband was not – and after a few years that became a big problem for me. He wasn't keen on getting a mortgage but for me, renting meant a life that was going nowhere. My dad had bought the house I grew up in with a mortgage, so that was what I wanted.

My husband had been at Arnhem, and afterwards I was told he was 'missing' for some time. [The battle of Arnhem in the Netherlands was a major World War II battle in September 1944.] So there was a lot of worry and uncertainty until he returned. In the war, I'd earned good money making overcoats for the Army in a factory above the menswear chain, Burton's, in Harrow.

We could have gone a long way really. We had no children. We were both working. But I wanted progress, a house of my own. I wanted that to go forward in life. He just wanted a good time.

So after six years of marriage I told him I wanted out: a divorce. Which was far from easy in those days but, in the end, he said he was willing to do it.

I had to go to the High Court to get the divorce, and it cost me £100, a lot of money at the time.

Before I went into the court the solicitor told me I had to say, "I want him back," over and over again.

The solicitor said, 'If you say you don't want him back you won't get the divorce.'

I'm an honest person but I did what the solicitor told me. If my husband had said he didn't want the divorce, I would not get it.

Six months later I got a call from my ex-husband's uncle. He said, 'He's not very happy,' – in other words, he wanted us to get together again.

My response was: 'Tell him TOUGH, I've been unhappy for SIX YEARS.'

After the divorce, it took a while but things got a little bit easier, and there were better jobs around. In the 1950s I applied for a new job at the GPO as a telephonist. The wages were £11 a week. I wrote off for the job but I didn't hear any more for ages.

Then suddenly the letter came in the post offering me the job.

When I told my boss, he said, 'You're a young woman, you can earn more, why shouldn't you go for it?'

But he closed the firm down a month later.

With the war and afterwards, I think what helped was

being able to talk to the girls at work; we could confide in each other in a way.

When you have nothing to lose, you're good to each other, you're all more or less in the same boat. Everyone supported each other. That's what it was.

Barbara remarried in the 1960s, a happy marriage which lasted for over forty years.

## THE ASSISTED PASSAGE SCHEME TO AUSTRALIA

FACTS about Assisted Passages to Australia (Australian News and Information Bureau, March 1955).

Australia is a British land short of people. A continent thirty-two times as large as the United Kingdom with a population of only nine millions, this young and growing member of the British Commonwealth is determined to increase her numbers by immigration as rapidly as economic conditions and opportunities of development exist. And she is anxious to maintain a high proportion of British Settlers in her total immigration programme.

These are reasons why Australia is following a policy of encouragement which has as its cornerstone an open invitation to British people anywhere in the

United Kingdom to take up life in Australia if they are interested in immigration.

Among more than 800,000 permanent new settlers from overseas since 1946 there have been as many British people as immigrants from all other countries added together.

About half of all British people arriving in Australia in this period travelled under the British Assisted Passages Scheme, the other half travelled at their own expense.

There is no limit to the number of British migrants who can be considered for assisted passages to Australia.

The above is a pamphlet issued by the Australian High Commission in 1955 to anyone interested in assisted emigration to Australia – for the princely sum of £10.

This, and a great deal of promotional material to encourage post-war Britons to up sticks and move to the other side of the world, was the idea Barbara and her friends at work discussed at length.

The assisted passage migration scheme was started by the Australian government in 1945; a similar New Zealand scheme was launched in 1947.

The scheme, initially known as the racist White Australia policy (the 'whites only' policy did not end until 1973), was intended to increase the white population of Australia and

New Zealand and supply workers for the booming industries there. Blacks or Asians need not apply.

Adult migrants would pay £10 to travel to Australia
or New Zealand; children of these migrants travelled free
of charge. In 1949, the value of £10 would be equivalent to
£355.70 in current terms. The UK average salary then was
just over £100 a year.

It was a hugely tempting idea; people were being promised jobs, affordable housing and a more optimistic lifestyle.
On arrival, migrants were housed in basic hostels. In those
early post-war years, many arrived in Australia in refitted
troop ships. Only later did the emigration scheme extend to
travel by air.

In the first year of the scheme, 400,000 British people
applied. Between 1945 and 1972 a million people had left
Britain's shores for Australia. Given the ongoing post-war
housing shortage and endless rationing, the prospect of an
optimistic new life in the sun continued to be popular for
many years. The UK scheme peaked in the 1960s and was
phased out in the 1980s.

The downside of the idea was that migrants were required
to remain in Australia for two years. If they wanted to leave
they would have to refund the cost of their assisted passage
to go home. Back then this was a huge sum, difficult to fork
out for most.

While those who had dreamed of a better life – wages in
the 1950s in Australia were 50 per cent higher than those in
the UK – decided to stay and make their life there, around

25 per cent of the assisted migrants returned to the UK. Around half of those returnees later came back to Australia – 'boomerang' emigration as it was known.

As Barbara Rivers clearly stated, that step into the unknown just after the war was a bold one – and at a time of no television and limited communication, other than letters from family or friends, not much was really known or understood about Australian life. And that included its climate, which could hit surprising extremes.

For some British arrivals, it was a shock too many. Post-war Australia seemed too big, desolate, even uncouth to those accustomed to life in the big cities many had left behind. Some Australians, in turn, were not all that keen on newcomers to the wide brown land, many of whom had never even been up close to an insect – let alone a flock of sheep. Yet others remained, took the plunge – and thrived.

History describes them as 'Ten Pound Poms'. (The word 'pom' is an abbreviated word for pomegranate, Aussie slang for immigrant.) Like most of the other migrants who arrived in Australia post-war, many newly arrived Poms found the new country a welcoming place.

## 'IT WAS A FUN TIME TO BE A KID'

London Zoo, in Regent's Park, was a long-time favourite for Winston Churchill. So when the news came in September 1947 that Churchill would be visiting the zoo, the popular newspapers were happy to oblige their readers. Churchill the lion tamer!

Amongst these readers was nine-year-old Chris Lambrianou, now living with his family in a council flat in east London.

For Londoners like Chris, the havoc of wartime had brought bombs, shelters and upheaval as his family, like everyone else, battled to cope. But now that was all over. And for some youngsters, the city itself, damaged and battered as it was, was a huge adventure playground.

My younger brother Tony and I loved London Zoo. Tony, two years younger, loved big cats. We'd read in the paper that Churchill was going down to the zoo and sure enough, we went there and actually saw 'Winnie' feeding his lion. The lion was called Rota, and apparently it was a gift given to him because of all his victories in North Africa.

There were loads of us all watching it. After that, Tony and I went off to have a ride on an elephant. To get into the zoo we did our favourite trick, we 'bumped' in. We knew that if you went round to the back of the zoo, some of the fences had come loose. But as little ones we could easily creep through and get in. [London Zoo had initially closed when war started but it reopened in 1939, complete with bomb shelters. Many people visited the zoo during the war – it was regarded as a public morale booster – with one and a half million visitors in 1943.]

Kids like us didn't worry about what had happened to us in the war. It might sound like we were quite daring, but it was just kids having fun, playing hide-and-seek in the shelters that were still all over the place. In many ways it was a fine time to be a kid.

Living where we did, close to many places, street markets, railway stations, there were lots of things we could go out and do. We'd get the number twenty-two bus from Homerton to Piccadilly. The bus fare was no problem for kids, as sometimes the bus conductor wouldn't want any money – they knew kids didn't have a lot of money. For all the damage and destruction everywhere then, there was still a great deal of kindness around now the war was over.

Old people, I remember, were very well respected then; they'd been there and done it all. If they were in any kind of trouble, people would come to help. And you always had a laugh with them, Cockney humour, that sort of thing. The war didn't destroy all that.

We'd even go out collecting things to earn a little bit of money. Tony and I would get a barrow for a shilling, it had long wooden handles and two big wheels. We'd take it out for five or six hours and go round collecting bottles, as you could get money for those. Another thing we did was to go down to the big railway stations like Liverpool Street and Victoria and offer to carry women's suitcases for a tip, usually a shilling or sixpence a time. At Victoria Coach Station, it was mainly women with suitcases who would come off the coach. We'd ask, 'Carry your bag, lady?' and they'd be pleased for us to do it – it's a straight walk down from the coach station to the main railway line.

The pictures was another place we'd often 'bump' into. I must have seen *Samson and Delilah* thirty times. [Released in 1949 with Victor Mature and Hedy Lamarr in the biblical roles, the film was a huge box-office success.]

We would just dash into the cinema; when someone came out of the back door, we'd be waiting there. As it opened we'd dive in. Once inside, we'd keep a look-out for the attendants or the ice-cream lady and creep into a seat without them spotting us.

Sometimes they'd spot us and chuck us out, but not that often.

I still remember what we'd eat at home. People were eating a lot of rabbit and pigeon, both affordable and not on the rations. My mum would make us our Sunday dinners with rabbit, and she'd also make pies like cheese and onion pie, apple pie, very inventive, which you had to be. Another thing was there were a lot of second-hand stalls on the markets around us, so people could buy all sorts of things on the cheap from there – and from the rag-and-bone man. [The rag-and-bone man, also known as a totter, went round collecting unwanted household goods to sell on. Historically, rag-and-bone men would work on foot but post-World War II they either used a handcart or a pony and cart.]

We were a close family. In the 1930s my mum had been a 'nippy' (a waitress who worked in the J. Lyons tea shops) in the big Lyons Corner House in Piccadilly. That's where she met my dad when he worked there as a chef. He was a fun dad, but always working long hours so we didn't see enough of him. When we kids were older, my mum cleaned offices in the City.

All we kids ever dreamed of at home was to be able to buy our mum a fur coat. Fur coats were a big thing then. All the posh women had them, women like the ones whose suitcases we'd carry. For years as I was growing up I'd say, 'Mum, I'm gonna buy you a fur coat.' But sadly, by the time I could afford it later on, my mum, Lilian, was gone.

Lilian had died of lung cancer as she'd been a heavy smoker; the men smoked Player's Navy Cut and the women smoked Player's Weights. She'd gone on her first-ever holiday up to County Durham, where her family came from. She collapsed and died in hospital up there. It was awful. My dad left us a long time later, in 1980. The thing about my parents was they never ever failed us children, they never let us down.

What you look back on most of all about that time, was the kindness you saw around you. It was always amongst the poorest people that you found it.

Those that had little would be happy to share it. People had good hearts.

As Christopher Lambrianou recalls, street markets in cities were good hunting grounds post-war for anyone with very little to spend. The government had sold off large quantities of wartime items at public auctions. This meant that all manner of army surplus goods came onto the market.

These could be all types of ex-Army clothing or larger items, for example parts from a plane. Smaller items like gas mask containers, folding bikes or Army penknives all found their way via auctions onto the cheap stalls. At one stage there were a handful of city shops selling Army surplus goods, electronic items and spares.

Some of it was junk. But for those willing to browse or looking out for anything cheap and electronic, for example spare parts for a radio, these outlets proved very useful.

## DESTROYING HITLER'S BUNKER

The war had ended. Britain and its Allies had celebrated victory over Germany, yet many of Britain's Armed Forces remained overseas, in various places in Europe – and often in a divided post-war Germany.

David Belfield was born in 1929 in Lincolnshire. As a teenager David volunteered for the Navy but was called up into the Army in February 1946, joining the Manchester Regiment. Since he was serving his time as a builder, he was transferred to the Royal

Engineers, training in bridge work and explosives. In 1947 he was sent off to what was initially an unknown destination.

'We sailed from Harwich to Holland, then we were sent to Berlin, arriving on Christmas Eve.

Our barracks were next door to Spandau Prison. [Spandau, located in the British Section of West Berlin, became notorious throughout the world because it housed seven Nazi war criminals who had been sentenced by the Allies during the Nuremberg Trials of 1945–6.]

I was in the 338 Construction Squadron. Our job was to destroy Hitler's bunkers.

We did this by boring holes into the walls, along the centre, and then filling them with explosives. This took us nearly twelve months and we thought we should be called the Destruction Squadron.

Berlin was divided (between the British, American, Soviet Union and French sectors of the city) and in 1948 the Russians imposed the Berlin blockade, sealing off all rail, road and canal routes upon which the city depended for food and fuel deliveries from the sectors occupied by the Western Allies. The Russians overlooked the possibility that West Berlin could be supplied by air and what was known as the Berlin Airlift started. We were involved in building runways and taxiways for the planes.

Berlin was devastated with so many buildings demolished. Women and girls picked up all the bricks and rubble, working all day, day in, day out, for rations of food like soup. The people were starving and literally had nothing. Any men available drove diggers with the rubble to the airfield to make runways.

The airfield was just fields with some wooden huts where there was a makeshift canteen.

It was a fantastic operation, as plane after plane arrived with supplies, one after the other. One day a plane had a burst tyre and blocked the runway. It was pushed out of the way immediately by a bulldozer to free the runway. [277,000 flights were made in total.]

We were paid in paper money with HM Forces stamped on it and this could only be spent in the NAAFI. Cigarettes were used for bartering on the black market. The ration was 110 cigarettes, a bar of soap and sweets or chocolate. I was also in Hamelin for two months, a beautiful town and the only place I saw that was untouched by the war.

Everywhere else was in rack and ruin.'

## BRITAIN'S FIRST SHOPPING REVOLUTION

Rationing and austerity might seem to be a way of life. Yet in 1948 a few stirrings in the high street would eventually transform everyday shopping.

One was the opening of a new shop in St Albans, Hertfordshire, spearheaded by a former market trader. He had started out with a stall in London's East End, a stall the young man had scraped together to buy with his demob money – after serving in World War I.

That single stall – ironically enough, selling off cheap World War I army surplus stock – developed into a number of market stalls, by then selling cheap, affordable foodstuffs through the 1920s.

By the 1930s, the stalls had morphed into a hundred grocery stores across the country and the word Tesco was established in food retailing.

Yet Tesco's founder, Jack Cohen, son of a Polish Jewish immigrant in London's East End, had spotted, in a visit to the US after the war, a truly revolutionary idea: a self-service food shop where customers would no longer have to wait to be served by a person behind the counter – now they could pick and choose whatever they wanted from the shelves.

Other self-service food shops were also launched that year – the Co-operative Society self-service shops opened in Manor Park, East London and in Southsea, Hampshire.

At first, people were reluctant to take on the new idea: shopping etiquette was very much ingrained in post-war culture, and grocery customers tended to have a strong relationship with anyone serving behind their local food counter. You might have to wait, but it was often a friendly exchange of words.

The idea that you didn't wait for someone to serve you but picked up the goods yourself seemed alien – some people worried that they'd be seen as a thief. Other shoppers felt the 'new' idea itself was anti-community. Yet as the idea gradually gathered momentum a year later, another established food retailer took the plunge – the first self-service Sainsbury's opened its doors in November 1950 and Britain's huge supermarket culture started to take root.

In a sense, that one humble market stall from an energetic ex-serviceman from the early twentieth century had thrown the first switch – directly into the country's supermarket phenomenon.

## *WINDRUSH*: THE ARRIVAL THAT CHANGED BRITAIN

It wasn't just Australia that was keen to encourage migration. Britain too needed post-war immigration to cover its employment shortages in state-run services like, for example, the railways.

The British Nationality Act of 1948 created the status of 'Citizens of the United Kingdom and its Colonies' and this allowed 800 million people from around the former colonial Empire-turned-Commonwealth an entitlement to settle in Britain.

On 22 June 1948 a former German cruise boat, the *Empire Windrush*, steamed into Tilbury Docks. On board were 500 settlers from Kingston, Jamaica.

Many were ex-servicemen who had served in England during the war. The newspapers had already alerted its readers to the voyage calling it 'the sons of Empire'. The colonial secretary of the time, Arthur Creech Jones, had already told the BBC, 'These people have British passports and they must be allowed to land,' given that other government departments openly viewed the arrival with much-raised eyebrows.

The tide of history was turning. But the shock of the arrival of 500 British passport-holding individuals who were not white-skinned was deeply embedded in the culture of Britain as it was then. As we have heard in previous chapters, nearly all foreigners from other countries were treated with suspicion after the war. So this news, at the time, seemed alarming. Michael Proom (see chapter 2) recalls the post-war attitudes.

The empire had always had a darker side, although at the time everyone in Britain either lived in genuine total ignorance of it, or just buried their heads in the sand. By today's standards we were all racists back then – one way or another. The postcolonial citizens of Australia, Canada and New Zealand were perfectly acceptable as equals, but then of course they were all white-skinned and mostly then of British stock. Perhaps the thinking of the day is best summed up by the common expression of the pre- and post-war years of 'play the white man, old chap' made by one Englishman to another when seeking fair play.

It was this into largely racist Britain that the first immigrants were disembarking from the islands of the Caribbean. Organisations like London Transport and Metropolitan Councils across the nation were desperate to fill lower jobs. Life was hard for this advance guard of what has since become Britain's multicultural society. They and their descendants had to confront almost a subsequent half-century of prejudice. Yet their arrival changed Britain forever.

## THE WELFARE STATE

There was, of course, another big arrival in Britain on 5 July 1948 – the arrival of the National Health Service.

Here's a brief snapshot of the year the NHS was launched.

- The UK population was just over 50 million.
- 94 per cent of the population enrolled with the NHS.
- Life expectancy was just over sixty-five for men, seventy for women.
- Many children were affected by rickets; heart disease and cancer were the most common causes of adult death.
- The average house price was £1,751 – though millions were still living in war-damaged homes, prefabs or sub-standard rented accommodation.
- Bread rationing had finally ended, and clothes had already been derationed earlier in the year.

What kind of healthcare existed before that, you might wonder?

There were insurance schemes, though they were very limited. The arrival of the 1911 National Insurance Act by the then Liberal government was a step forward at the time because it did insure employed workers in some industries were covered for a doctor's visit, but not for hospital treatment.

Other health insurance schemes of the time were linked to certain funds and clubs which working people could pay into.

There were charities, and a number of public hospitals across the country. The wealthy would pay and receive good treatment from specialist consultants – but far too many poorer people relied solely on charity if they fell ill, or a kindly local doctor who didn't charge. Failing that, poor people would often rely on folklore remedies.

Even by 1948, families could not afford medicines at all, although they might have been prescribed by a doctor. So many would resort to using cheap, popular remedies, handed down for generations. Here are a few, some of which could be bought at a chemist or dispensary:

- Syrup of figs (for constipation)
- Castor oil (for constipation and high temperature)
- Carter's Little Liver Pills (a laxative)
- Treacle and brimstone (for a bad chest: brimstone is a form of sulphur)

- Brandy for toothaches (placed on the gum on cotton wool).
- Andrews Liver Salt (for constipation and temperature)
- Milk of Magnesia (for tummy problems, e.g. heartburn)
- Derbac soap (for head lice)
- Germolene (for cuts and grazes)
- Almond oil (for softening ear wax)
- Dock leaf (for nettle stings)
- Snowfire (for chilblains)
- Spit (to be used on warts and rubbed on the bridge of the nose to clear the sinuses).

In the 1930s, Frank Mee's family in the north-east could afford a nominal sum for healthcare, but it was very carefully thought out.

'My mother would pay a weekly sum into the local doctor's surgery. It was not a lot but it meant that the family was on the doctor's 'panel' [a panel meant that a GP could take on private and panel patients, and essentially the wealthier private fees charged would subsidise the GP's fee for the poorer "panel" patients]. When sent for, the doctor would arrive and expect a half-crown put in his hand before he stepped into the house. So we always called them 'the half-crown doctors'. [Half a crown is equivalent to two shillings and sixpence, roughly £4.50 today]. He would prescribe the medication (usually in his big black bag) and my mother would pay for the drugs.'

## THE ARRIVAL OF THE NHS

'Doctors and people collaborate today in a tremendous social experiment' claimed the *Daily Express* newspaper on that auspicious July day. 'The new National Health scheme is launched. Wish it success.'

It had been a protracted and perilous birth. Bringing free medical services for everyone in the country was a radical idea – hence the 'social experiment' phrase.

The then health minister, Aneurin Bevan, had spent three years to get the free health service up and running – and its future had often seemed uncertain.

Bevan had to deploy strong political skills to negotiate the NHS' birth, since he was determined that the new health service would 'universalise the best' and not just be a safety net for poor people. It had to be free to all.

He faced eighteen months of bitter resistance from the British Medical Association which did not like the plan. The doctors disliked the idea that they should become, in some degree, servants of the state.

Bevan's strategy was to split the profession. He won over the hospital consultants by agreeing they could use certain NHS 'pay beds' for private care. Then he withdrew his proposals to force GPs into a salaried service.

Back in 1942, as previously cited, Sir William Beveridge had set down his vision of post-war Britain in a widely read report, eliminating the five great evils plaguing society: disease, want, ignorance, squalor and idleness.

The end of war, the report stated, would restructure Britain's society in two ways: first with National Insurance and secondly with the National Health Service. Now, with the war over, Clement Attlee's Labour Party were ushering in Beveridge's proposals.

National Insurance, introduced in 1911 by the then Liberal government, had been, technically, the kick-start of Britain's welfare state, providing protection against life's hardships for the old or unemployed, i.e. for those least able to help themselves.

Yet the 1948 launch of the National Insurance was far more comprehensive. It covered the entire population. The payment of a weekly insurance 'stamp' as it was commonly known, gave the right to unemployment, disablement, sickness benefits, old-age pensions, widows' and orphans' pensions as well as maternity benefits, family allowances, and industrial injuries benefits.

The cost was divided: 20 per cent contributed by the insured person, 30 per cent by his or her employer, 50 per cent by the state. Here was a system of social security for the entire community.

Today, like income tax, National Insurance contributions are deducted at source from people's earnings. They are then paid into The National Insurance Fund, part of which is allocated to the NHS, and the rest is for funding other benefits. There are different classes of National Insurance with different amounts due to be paid. Some NI contributions are paid by self-employed people, and some can even be paid on a voluntary basis – to fill any gaps in the contributor's record.

But what of those who started working in the NHS as it was then? How did they feel about the new system?

At St Thomas' Hospital in London, where charity had been provided freely or under charitable auspices for many centuries, the date of the arrival of the NHS was greeted with great excitement.

Student nurses in casualty had, in the past, been required to explain to patients that the hospital depended on voluntary contributions, rattling little tin boxes on their desks to emphasise the point. Rattling these boxes to frequently shabbily dressed and poverty-stricken patients was always embarrassing for the nurses.

Now it was over. One day, before the official opening of the NHS, the nurses and their colleagues ceremoniously threw out the little tin boxes. A new day was coming. For everyone.

## AN NHS NURSE IN THE 1950S

Margaret was born in 1936 and enjoyed a career in nursing for forty-three years. Her training started in 1952, a few years after the NHS was launched. She retired at the age of sixty.

On Empire Day, a celebration when the British ruled over their empire, schoolchildren would be dressed up in the various national costumes and clothes depicting the various occupations of the people of the British Isles.

At six, I was 'the nurse', resplendent in my white cap and apron with a very large red cross on my chest, carrying a doll, suitably bandaged.

I'd had a chequered school life because of the war. By thirteen I had moved to nine different schools, but on every Empire Day, no matter where, I was always dressed up as 'the nurse'. [Empire Day become Commonwealth Day in 1949 and ceased to be a public holiday in 1966.]

Leaving school, I was asked by the careers officer what I was going to do. My reply, that I was going to be a nurse, was met with disapproval, including the headmaster who felt that I should be a teacher and not waste my abilities on a 'low paid, dirty job'.

However, I got an interview with the matron and was accepted to start my nurse training. At first I did some months as a cadet nurse in the hospital: this was fetching and carrying patients, X-rays and documents from and to the various departments. Then I started my nurse training in September 1952: three months in training school learning hospital etiquette, anatomy, physiology, hygiene and psychology, day after day. There was no academic level to be reached before entering nursing. As a grammar school girl I was used to studying and did not find the work as difficult as some of my colleagues with a less formal education. Everyone had a chance to succeed if they wanted to be a nurse. There were sixteen in the training school. Only one failed the course.

At the end of training, we were allowed on the wards. We were given bright pink dresses and were therefore referred to as 'Pinkies'.

Tynemouth Victoria Jubilee Infirmary in North Shields and Preston Hospital (since closed in the mid-90s) were then separate hospitals, and when we left training we went back to our own hospital.

Eleven of us went to Preston. We arrived on the wards packed full of knowledge.

We realised in the first hour that we knew nowt!

We learned slowly by example and practical teaching, sometimes by a nurse just a few months' training ahead of us. Or by a staff nurse. My first ward was Female Surgical and the very experienced sister gave me some good advice on my first day: 'Keep your eyes wide open and your mouth tight shut.'

The training was hard, a fifty-seven-hour week, half a day off once a fortnight. The pay was seven pounds, nine shillings a month. My nurse's home – with my own 'cell' – was home for the next two years. All our meals were provided and uniforms, so the only expense was black shoes and stockings.

There was little social life as we were always so tired. We were checked in by 10.30pm or 11pm – and that was a late pass, only allocated with Matron after special interview. Nurses in training were not to marry until they qualified and again, only after Matron's permission. Only two of the sisters on the ward were married, and most had a Queen Alexandra Nursing background, many with active war service.

The discipline spilled over the many aspects of our daily routine. You addressed all consultants as 'Sir', we went 'on leave' not holiday and asked permission to come and go off duty.

The ward sister did a full round to each patient each morning and before she went off duty at night, and was always available for visitors during 7.00–7.30pm visiting hours. She knew all about every patient, their illness, and woe betide a sister or staff nurse who didn't have the name and diagnosis of every patient ready for the matron's ward round, at 11am daily.

I qualified as a State Registered Nurse in 1957, so I became a staff nurse on a busy male surgical ward, extremely busy with five consultants and operations carried out daily, plus we were on surgical call on alternate weekends. The ward sister was ex-Army and had served in Crete. She was wonderful and the men loved and responded to her. She taught me how to handle people. She was a born nurse and did it so well.

She could have a bank manager in one bed and a vagrant in another, and both would feel that the most important thing she had to do that day was look after both of them. She was a wonderful example, respected by all the doctors and consultants alike.

In 1961 I was given my first post as a ward sister on a children's ward of twenty-one beds. The children were from birth to age sixteen and suffering from chronic illness, kidney disease, casualty trauma from road accidents and other general surgical conditions. I was there for four years and in that time had four cases of leukaemia. At that time, despite treatment and multiple transfusions, the little patients all died. Not like today when 90 per cent are cured.

One little seven-year-old, whom we had nursed many times during his short life, came in yet again for a further blood transfusion. He was on a drip for four days and all his veins had collapsed. Life for him had become unbearable. I was there beside his mother when he begged her not to let them give him any more blood.

We watched this pale little boy ebbing away, but with such courage. His mother and I just held each other, and cried together in the corridor outside his room.

I explained the consequences to her when she told me to take the drip down, but she understood it all far better than I, or the doctors, could possibly have done. He died peacefully at 5am the following morning. I will never forget him.

There was the other side of the coin. I remember one man who fell forty feet into a dock, bouncing on the stagings as he fell. Multiple fractures and an amputated left foot. The pelvis was shattered. This resulted in a ruptured bowel and bladder. I went to the operating

285

theatre with him that evening. [A staging location or area is a common choice for an outbound shipping dock.]

There were five surgeons operating, and twenty-three pints of plasma and eleven pints of blood went into him in a five-hour operation. He was a very ill man for some time but twelve months later he walked out of the hospital on his own two feet. This is what it means to be part of it. I received a Christmas card from him for the next twenty-one years until he died of a heart attack, aged seventy-one.

After twenty-six years' nursing in hospitals, in the late 1970s I left to become a community district nursing sister in Newcastle. I had very good and supportive colleagues in the district, willing to help if I was stumped. I thoroughly enjoyed my years doing that, with great support from the five doctors I worked for.

People often ask if I have liked one aspect of nursing more than the other, but they were each so different. In hospital, the hierarchy is the patient at the bottom, then the ward sister, then the consultant. In a patient's home it's the opposite, with doctor, then the sister, then the patient. As the sister you are a guest in their home, though you can advise and liaise with the doctor about their treatment.

I don't regret leaving hospital nursing when I did, because there were many changes. In my time there has always been a shortage of nurses, mostly caused by low pay and increased academic entrance standards. In the 1960s we accepted the management changes which meant fewer staff and pairs of hands on the wards. Each government has shuffled this around.

When I retired, in the community set-up we had just a shared staff nurse and a part-time enrolled nurse as well as a twenty-hour auxiliary nurse – all to nurse between 12,000 and 14,000 patients.

Life was crazily busy and very stressful. Nevertheless I've no regrets about my nursing career – you live with your memories of those fulfilling years.

As Alan Everett pointed out in an earlier chapter, until the arrival of the NHS many people were reluctant to call for a doctor who could charge them a sum of money. Most likely, it would be a woman who would be dealing with anything and everything at home: births, deaths, coughs and sneezes, toothache or childhood ailments. So the new health service had an immediate impact on women of all ages. Frequently, their own ailments had been neglected as they were seen as too expensive to treat.

Female GPs in the poorer districts were overwhelmed by the difference in the numbers of cases, even in the first six months after July 1948. Women flooded into the doctors' surgeries with their ailments. Suddenly, they could be treated.

Margaret Powell (1907–84) had been a domestic servant for much of her early life. In later life she wrote a series of popular books about domestic service which were the inspiration for TV series like *Downton Abbey* and *Upstairs Downstairs*. She noted in her book *Climbing the Stairs* that the hospital experience for a patient changed dramatically in 1948.

She said her first experience of hospital in 1944 had been nasty. The food and amenities were 'deplorable', the lack of privacy distressing. In 1948 she was hospitalised again with breast cancer.

'What a change I found,' she wrote.

'You were treated as though you mattered. The bed I'd had before was like lying on the pebbles on Brighton beach. But now I had a rubber mattress. I felt as though I could have lain there forever.'

\* \* \*

History now tells us that the events outlined in these pages, of the post-war years of 1945–8, proved to have all manner of consequences for many generations to come.

It is no secret that the country stumbled, time and again, in the years after the end of World War II, only to recover for set periods, then stumble again, a see-saw effect that continues even today.

Significantly, however, the core of the ideas put forward to the country in a report generated in 1942 (by Sir William Beveridge) was retained: Britain still has a welfare state and a National Health Service, both continuously under fire in recent years but, in the case of the NHS, held aloft, time and again, with great esteem and pride by the people of the UK. Politics aside, that is a remarkable show of faith and support.

But what else of Britain's people, dancing for sheer joy, embracing each other and hugging total strangers on VE Day, overwhelmingly grateful that their lives and those of their allies could now enjoy, once again, the freedoms that had been so bitterly fought for?

Certainly, friendships forged out of shared common experiences in war have proved to be enduring. The country is still very much a land of voluntary helpers, which is also easily observed by the many millions raised for the NHS in 2020 by the World War II veteran, Captain Tom Moore, tirelessly walking the length of his garden – at nearly one hundred years old.

Our love of country, so strong in wartime, has not been, perhaps, as clearly defined as it once was. It's been said that Britain is always too bashful about patriotism. Brits don't, as a rule, admire the boaster. And respect for King and country was a hallmark of the pre-World War II years. It was bound to evaporate somewhat with successive generations.

Yet what cannot be questioned in this day and age is the sense of unity and community that prevailed in the country's darkest days, yet has emerged anew in the present. Strong qualities that kept the country going even at the worst point.

'I have never in my life seen so united a people,' commented US politician Wendell Willkie back in 1940.

The connection from 1945 to 2020 might not be self-evident at times. Yet it is still the very spirit of the people, and the qualities of quiet endurance and stoicism, so crucial then, that have prevailed.

These qualities have stood fast. And that is why the story recounted on these pages is so important.

# SOURCES AND BIBLIOGRAPHY

## CHAPTER 1

Excerpts from Joan Strange's diary, taken from Strange, Joan and McCooey, Chris (ed.), *Despatches* [sic] *from the Home Front: The War Diaries of Joan Strange*, Tunbridge Wells, Jak Books, 1989, new edn 2013

Excerpts from Eva Merrill's memoir: *Merrill, Eva, Looking Back: Reflections of a London Child in the War Years 1939-1945*, Author House Publishing, 2013

Excerpts from Joan Blackburn's memoir: *Blackburn, Joan, Granddad's Rainbow, Adventures of a War Baby 1939-51*, Woodfield Publishing, 2010

Excerpts from Kathleen Wilson's memoir, *International Service*, Queenspark Books, Brighton, 2002

Excerpts from Lesley and Terence Spencer's memoir, *Living Dangerously*, Percival Publications, 2012

Excerpts from Joe Roddis's diary (with Mark Hillier), *In Support of the Few*, Yellowman Ltd, 2013

## CHAPTER 2

Excerpts from Doris Grimsley, taken from author's personal interview

Excerpts from Karen Steele, taken from author's personal interview

Excerpts from Joan Blackburn's memoir: *Grandad's Rainbow, Adventures of a War Baby 1939-51*, Woodfield Publishing, 2010

Excerpts from Frank Mee, taken from author's personal interview

Excerpts from Christopher Lambrianou, taken from author's personal interview

Excerpts from Michael Proom's memoir: *Orpington 127, The Autobiography of a War Baby*, Grosvenor House Publishing, 2013

## CHAPTER 3

Excerpts from Ron Piper's memoir, *Take Him Away*, Queenspark Books, Brighton, 1995

Excerpts from Judy Williams, taken from author's personal interview

Excerpts from Frank Mee, taken from author's personal interview

## CHAPTER 4

Excerpts from Yvonne Gough-Macdonald, taken from author's personal interview

Excerpts from Roy Pryor, taken from author's personal interview

Excerpts from Ivy Gardiner, taken from author's personal interview

Excerpts from Frank Mee, taken from author's personal interview

Excerpts from Joy Beebe memoir, *Snapshots of a War Bride's Life*, Beebe Publishing, 2012

Excerpts from Vera Barber, taken from author's personal interview

## CHAPTER 5

Excerpts from Fred Roberts memoir, *Duxford to Karachi, an RAF Armourer's War*, Victory Books, 2006

Excerpts from Joan Blackburn's memoir, *Grandad's Rainbow, Adventures of a War Baby, 1939-51*, Woodfield Publishing, 2010

Excerpts from Roy Pryor, taken from author's personal interview

Excerpts from Philip Gunyon, taken from author's personal interview

Excerpts from Marjory Batchelor, taken from her memoir, *A Life Behind Bars*, Queenspark Books, 1999

Excerpts from Alan Everett's memoir, *Corned Beef City, An Autobiography of a Kid from Dagenham*, Amazon Kindle.

## CHAPTER 6

Excerpts from Kathleen Wilson's memoir, *International Service*, Queenspark Books, Brighton, 2002

Excerpts from Michael Proom's memoir, *Orpington 127, The Autobiography of a War Baby*, Grosvenor House Publishing, 2013.

Excerpts from Joan Blackburn's memoir, *Grandad's Rainbow, Adventures of a War Baby, 1939-51*, Woodfield Publishing, 2010

Excerpts from Dave Dutton's memoir, *The Thirty Bob Kid, The Autobiography of a Northern Bastard.* CreateSpace Independent Publishing, 2018

Excerpts from Jennifer Wright, taken from author's personal interview

## CHAPTER 7

Excerpts from Barbara Rivers, taken from author's personal interview

Excerpts from Christopher Lambrianou, taken from author's personal interview

Excerpts from Michael Proom's memoir, *Orpington 127, The Autobiography of a War Baby*, Grosvenor House, Publishing, 2013.

## OTHER SOURCES

(See also 'Recommended reading')

Gardiner, Juliet, *Wartime Britain 1939-1945*, Headline Publishing, 2005

Kynaston, David, *Austerity Britain 1945-51*, Bloomsbury, 2008

Waller, Maureen, *London 1945*, John Murray, 2005

Nicholson, Virginia, *Millions Like Us, Women's Lives During the Second World War*, Penguin Books, 2012

Longmate, Norman, *How We Lived Then*, Pimlico, 2002

Yorke, Trevor, *The 1930s House Explained*, Countryside Books, 2006

BBC WW2 People's War online archive (www.bbc.co.uk/history/ww2peopleswar/)

*Best of British Magazine* (www.bestofbritishmag.co.uk) and *Yesterday Remembered* (www.yesterdayremembered.co.uk/)

Remembering the Past (memoriesnorthtyne.org.uk)

Renfrewshire Libraries (libcat.renfrewshire.gov.uk)

Bolton Libraries (www.bolton.gov.uk)

Voices of Post War England (voicesofpostwarengland.wordpress.com)

*The Times*, *Daily Express*, *Daily Mirror*

## RECOMMENDED READING

Nicholson, Virginia, *Millions Like Us, Women's Lives During the Second World War*, Penguin Books, 2012

Panter-Downes, Mollie, *London War Notes*, Persephone Books, 2017

Waller, Maureen, *London 1945*, John Murray, 2005

David Kynaston, *Austerity Britain 1945-51*, Bloomsbury, 2008

Gardiner, Juliet, *Wartime Britain 1939-1945*, Headline, 2005

Hodgson, Vere, *Few Eggs and No Oranges, the Diaries 1940-1945*, reprinted Persephone Books, 2017

Telfer, Kevin, *The Summer of 1945, Voices from VE Day to VJ Day*, Aurum Press, 2015

# ACKNOWLEDGEMENTS

The truly valiant Inge and Paul Sweetman, Suzanne, Isobel and Holly at City Books in Hove deserve special recognition for their ongoing support and supply through the stormy days. Many thanks, as always, to the staff at Jubilee Library, Hove Library and the Westminster Reference Library.

The immensely supportive team at Bexley Library, especially Will Cooban, Susan Prior, Caroline Dennis and Margot Crook. Yet again, their efforts and enthusiasm are always much appreciated.

Dr. Kath Smith, of Remembering the Past and Bridging the Gap Tyneside, Chris McCooey, Frank Mee, Phil Gunyon, Christopher Lambrianou, Simon Stabler of Yesterday Remembered, the Everett family, Bev Clark, Vera Barber and the wonderful Eva Merrill (who sadly died, age 93, in April 2020) all gave valuable assistance, as did Doris Grimsley, Karen Steele, Cara Spencer, Janet Cowan, Jenny Wright and Judy Chester. Much appreciation also goes to Dave Dutton, Joan Blackburn and Michael Proom for their kind collaboration.

# ABOUT THE AUTHOR

JACKY HYAMS is a freelance journalist and non-fiction author. She has written several non-fiction books, many of them published by John Blake Publishing.

Her memoir *Bombsites and Lollipops: My 1950s East End Childhood*, published in 2011, and its follow-up, *White Boots & Miniskirts: A True Story of Life in the Swinging Sixties*, published in 2013, are highly acclaimed social histories of Britain's post-war era.

More recently, *The Day War Broke Out*, her story of how British families faced the Second World War together, was published in 2019 and her revised study of Britain's munitions workers, *Bomb Girls: the unsung heroines of the Second World War* was published in 2020.